Child poverty in large families

Child poverty in large families

Jonathan Bradshaw, Naomi Finch, Emese Mayhew, Veli-Matti Ritakallio and Christine Skinner

JOSEPH ROWNTREE
FOUNDATION

First published in Great Britain in June 2006 by

The Policy Press
Fourth Floor, Beacon House
Queen's Road
Bristol BS8 1QU
UK

Tel no   +44 (0)117 331 4054
Fax no   +44 (0)117 331 4093
Email   tpp-info@bristol.ac.uk
www.policypress.org.uk

© University of York 2006

Published for the Joseph Rowntree Foundation by The Policy Press

10-digit ISBN 1 86134 876 2
13-digit ISBN 978 1 86134 876 0

British Library Cataloguing in Publication Data
A catalogue record for this book is available from the British Library.

Library of Congress Cataloging-in-Publication Data
A catalog record for this book has been requested.

Jonathan Bradshaw is Professor of Social Policy, **Naomi Finch** is Research Fellow, **Emese Mayhew** is Research Assistant and **Christine Skinner** is Lecturer in Social Policy, all at the Social Policy Research Unit, University of York, UK. **Veli-Matti Ritakallio** is Professor of Social Policy at the University of Turku, Finland.

The **Joseph Rowntree Foundation** has supported this project as part of its programme of research and innovative development projects, which it hopes will be of value to policy makers, practitioners and service users. The facts presented and views expressed in this report are, however, those of the authors and not necessarily those of the Foundation.

Cover design by Qube Design Associates, Bristol
Cover photograph kindly supplied by www.alamy.co.uk
Printed in Great Britain by Latimer Trend Printing Group, Plymouth

Contents

List of figures and tables

Figures

Tables

Acknowledgements

We are grateful to the members of our project advisory committee:

Helen Barnard, Joseph Rowntree Foundation, who was also our research liaison officer
Professor Richard Berthoud, University of Essex
Dr Paul Dornan, Child Poverty Action Group
Professor Kathleen Kiernan, University of York
Francis McGlone, Save the Children, UK
Professor Eithne McLaughlin, Queen's University Belfast
Dr Tess Ridge, University of Bath

We are also grateful to Professor Holly Sutherland at the University of Essex who
undertook some policy simulations using POLIMOD.

Summary

Background

The abolition of child poverty is key to the UK government's social policy strategy. In 1999 the Prime Minister's Toynbee Hall speech promised 'to eradicate child poverty within a generation'. Child poverty is associated with poor child well-being and well-becoming. For a child to be poor just because they live in a large family is a particular injustice. This is already recognised to some extent in the tax and benefit system, which varies payments for families with different numbers of children.

This study is based on secondary analysis of national and international data. The national data sets included the Family Resources Survey, the Millennium Cohort Study and the Families and Children Survey. The international data was drawn from the European Community Household Panel and the Luxembourg Income Study. The study also draws on national and international data on how the tax and benefit system impacts on model families.

Large families

What is a large family? In this study we have defined large families pragmatically – where it is possible, families with four or more children (4+ child families) (10% of all children) and otherwise, families with three or more children (3+ child families) (30% of all children). Over the last 60 years there has been a reduction in the proportion of families with three or more children. However, in 2004/05 children from such families represented 42% of all poor children. If the government is going to meet its target to eradicate child poverty in a generation, its family policy measures need to be extended more successfully to large families than at present.

Tax and benefit system

UK policies are not particularly sensitive to the needs of large families:

- Child Benefit (CB) is paid at a higher rate for the first child in a family.
- The Family Premium in Income Support (IS) effectively results in there being a premium for the first child in a family receiving IS.
- Working Tax Credit is paid at a standard rate regardless of the number of children.
- Child Tax Credit (CTC) is a standard amount for each child (except that there is a premium for a disabled child). However, the uprating of CTC has benefited large families more because the child rate has been increased in line with earnings while the family element has been frozen.
- The Child Support Agency (CSA) formula allows 17% of the income of a non-resident parent for the first child, 20% for the second child and 25% for the third *and subsequent children*.
- Childcare Tax Credit allows 70% of the costs of regulated childcare for *up to two children only*.

The study explores how the treatment of large families in the tax and benefit system has changed over time:

- The net income of an employed 3+ child family on average earnings relative to a childless couple has fallen since 1972.
- The net income of an employed 3+ child family on half average earnings has improved relative to a childless couple but stayed the same relative to a one-child family since 1972.
- The net income of an unemployed 3+ child family on IS, relative to both a childless couple and a one-child couple, has improved since 1988.

However, this does not mean that the 'implied equivalence scale' in the tax and benefit system is adequate or correct.

Child poverty in large families

Fifty per cent of children in 4+ child families are poor compared with only 23% in one-child families. Children in 3+ child families constitute 42% of all poor children. However, child poverty in large families has been falling since 1998/99. This could be the result of improvements in the employment rates in large families since then but we think that it is more likely to be due to the impact of Working Families' Tax Credit and CTC.

The characteristics of poor children in large families

This study employs three data sets to explore the characteristics of large families. From these we can conclude that children in large families are more likely to have a parent who:

- is not in employment;
- is from a minority ethnic group – particularly Pakistani or Bangladeshi;
- had their first child at a young age;
- has a preschool child in the household;
- has a low level of educational attainment;
- lives in London or Northern Ireland;
- is disabled.

Now all of these characteristics are also associated with a higher risk of child poverty. So the question arises: are children in large families more likely to be poor because of these characteristics or is there a 'large family effect' independent of them?

To answer this question we undertook statistical analysis to assess whether having taken account of these other factors there was still a higher child poverty rate in large families. All three data sets produced similar results – there is indeed a large family effect independent of the other characteristics of the families. A child in a 3+ child family is between 50% and 180% more likely than a one-child family to be poor, and a child in a 4+ child family is between 280% and 800% more likely to be poor than a one-child family – other things being equal.

International comparisons

All countries except Denmark in the original 15 European Union countries in 2001 have a higher child poverty rate in 3+ child families than in one-child families. The UK has the third highest child poverty rate in 3+ child families, only less than Spain and Portugal. The UK also has one of the biggest gaps between the poverty rate for children in one- and three-child families. This is partly because the UK benefit system is less successful in reducing child poverty in three-child families than it is in one-child families.

These analyses were replicated for 23 countries using the Luxembourg Income Study circa 2000 (1999 for the UK). Among these countries the UK has the second highest child poverty rate in 3+ families before benefits are taken into account, only Hungary had a higher rate. After benefits are taken into account the UK has the 10th highest child poverty rate. The UK reduces its child poverty rate in 3+ child families by the fourth highest amount but it is less successful in reducing its child poverty in 3+ child families than in one-child families.

These comparative analyses using two independent data sets show that the UK has one of the highest pre-transfer poverty rates for children in large families compared to other countries. It appears that the UK is middling in the generosity of the benefit package to large families. However, starting from a relatively high pre-transfer rate, UK policy is fairly effective in reducing its large family child poverty rate. However, the UK is not the most generous country, and children in large families still experience greater risks of poverty than their counterparts in smaller families. Thus, the UK is doing relatively well for its large families, but could do better.

Comparing Child Benefit packages

We drew on two comparative studies of the impact of the CB package on families of different sizes. Drawing on a study of 22 countries as at July 2001 we found that the CB package in the UK, while it is relatively generous to a one-child family, is far less generous to a 3+ child family at average earnings. Ireland and especially the UK pay comparatively higher CB packages to one-child families than 3+ child families. However, Belgium, France, Germany, Israel, Italy, New Zealand and Portugal pay higher amounts for the third (and subsequent) child.

This study has been replicated for 15 countries as at January 2004. Countries are making rather different judgements about the relative needs of families of different sizes. Austria is more generous for the third child and so are Belgium, the Netherlands and Sweden to a lesser extent. Australia is more generous to the second child and the UK is still unusual in favouring the first child.

How might child poverty in large families be reduced?

The Child Poverty Review announced 'a long term aspiration to improve the financial support available to large families'. Long-term implies that it will be achieved by gearing benefit rates towards larger families over a period of years. How might the government achieve this and at what cost? We use a micro simulation model of the tax and benefit system – POLIMOD with the assistance of Professor Holly Sutherland from the University of Essex – to attempt to answer these questions. Six policy changes were simulated:

The best outcome in terms of equity for large families is achieved by increasing Child benefit (CB) to the same level per child and then increasing the benefit for the third and subsequent child by £20 per week. However, it would cost £3.39 billion. Lesser increases in CB for larger families achieve more modest reductions in the poverty rates but at lower costs.

Adjustments in Child Tax Credit (CTC) to pay the same amount for each child cost less and achieve good results for large families. There are a number of potential cost-free solutions but reductions in the child poverty rate of large families for most of these are paid for by losses for small and/or better-off families. Also, because lone parents tend to be small families, they tend to suffer slight increases in child poverty rates.

These results illustrate that policy makers seeking to help large families face trade-offs of three kinds:

• About half of all poor children live in one- or two-child families and any policy which helps large families at the expense of small families is likely to result in an increase in child poverty in small families and also probably lone parent families and thus also possibly an increase in child poverty overall.
• There is of course a trade-off between the effectiveness of the policy in terms of equity and the cost to the Exchequer.
• There are also choices to be made between universal and selective policy measures. Improvements in CB for large families are expensive because they go to every large family whatever their income. Manipulating CTC for large families may concentrate extra help on those who need it most. However, CTC suffers from non-take-up and such measures will also increase the poverty trap (by incurring high marginal tax rates as earnings rise).

In any case a factor that might also be an important constraint on policy is the general public's views about the deserts of large families and/or the actual or believed behavioural or fertility effects of paying enhanced benefits to large families. An enhanced benefit for one-child families may raise fewer objections because every family with a child has at least one child. However, if enhanced benefits are to be paid for the third and subsequent child, smaller (and childless) families may object. There will certainly be arguments about the relative needs of families with different numbers of children and probably also anxiety expressed about the extent to which such premiums might be encouraging 'irresponsible' childbirth. However, as things are now, the challenge is why are small families so privileged in the tax and benefit system?

Glossary

AHC	after housing costs
BHC	before housing costs
CB	Child Benefit
CSA	Child Support Agency
CTB	Council Tax Benefit
CTC	Child Tax Credit
DWP	Department for Work and Pensions
ECHP	European Community Household Panel
FaCS	Families and Children Study
FRS	Family Resources Survey
GCSE	General Certificate of Secondary Education
HB	Housing Benefit
HBAI	Households Below Average Income
IS	Income Support
ISER	Institute for Social and Economic Research
JRF	Joseph Rowntree Foundation
JSA	Jobseeker's Allowance
LIS	Luxembourg Income Study
MCS	Millennium Cohort Study
OECD	Organisation for Economic Co-operation and Development
ONS	Office for National Statistics
POLIMOD	A micro-simulation model of the tax and benefit system.
PSE	Poverty and Social Exclusion
PSI	Policy Studies Institute
RPI	Retail Price Index
SILC	Survey of Income and Living Conditions
WFTC	Working Families' Tax Credit

Introduction

The abolition of child poverty is key to the UK government's social policy strategy. In 1999 the Prime Minister's Toynbee Hall speech promised 'to eradicate child poverty within a generation'. Subsequently the Treasury set out further objectives: to eradicate child poverty by 2020, to halve it by 2010 and 'to make substantial progress towards eliminating child poverty by reducing the number of children in poverty by at least a quarter by 2004' (HM Treasury, 2000).[1]

The Joseph Rowntree Foundation (JRF) published a review of evidence on *Ladders out of poverty* (Kemp et al, 2004). This concluded that one of the drivers (or snakes) leading to child poverty was living in a large family. This report was the result of a project on child poverty in large families (see Box 1), which was included in the programme of research that the JRF funded as a result of that review. The work is based on the secondary analysis of national and international data.

Box 1: What is a large family?

There is no formal or official definition. In this study we have been somewhat pragmatic – depending on the nature and availability of information on family size provided by the different data sets used in this study, we have selected families containing three or more/four or more children. However, two things should be noted:

(1) All the analysis in this report is cross-sectional – it is an analysis of a snapshot of families at a point in time. Some of the 'small' families were larger because they will have contained more children who have now left home or will become large families as more children are born. Also not all the children will be natural children of the parents. Some will be the result of repartnerings of parents who have brought children from previous partnerships and may have also had some from the new partnership. Willitts and Swales (2003) found that almost a fifth (18%) of large families were stepfamilies, compared to 9% of small families. A quarter of all large couple families were stepfamilies. Some large families will include children that are fostered and adopted. So we are not presenting a picture of fertility outcomes.

(2) The definition of children used is one in common statistical practice in the UK – a child under the age of 16 or aged 16-18 and in full-time education. A justification for this definition is that the statutory school leaving age is 16 and after that children can be in employment – that is, become tax units in their own right. However, increasingly, children over 16 are not in employment and whether they are or not they may well be dependent to some extent on their parents. So some of our 'small' families will have children in their households who are

continued.../

---

[1] The wording of the target was then altered: 'To reduce the number of children in low-income households by at least a quarter by 2004 as a contribution towards the broader target of halving child poverty by 2010 and eradicating it by 2020.... The target for 2004 will be monitored by reference to the number of children in low-income households by 2004/5. Low-income households are defined as households with income below 60 per cent of the median as reported in the HBAI statistics.... Progress will be measured against the 1998/9 baseline figures and methodology' (HM Treasury, 2002).

not counted as dependent children – although they may be dependent to some extent. Berthoud and Iavocou (2006) have used the data in the Family Resources Survey to create a fuller picture of patterns of family size.

Table 1 shows the distribution of the number of children in a household of families with children, first using the standard definition of a dependent child. It can be seen that the most common family size is the one with two children and that less than 3% have five or more and 0.75% have six or more children. When we add all children living in the household under the age of 25 an extra 4.5 million 'children' are added and there are now a higher proportion of one-child families and a higher proportion of families with four or more children.

Table 1: Distribution of dependent children in families by size[1]

Family size	Dependent children[2]		Children aged under 25[3]	
	%	Numbers	%	Numbers
1-child family	21.2	2,381,580	22.3	3,524,591
2-child family	45.8	5,155,542	43.7	6,905,206
3-child family	22.6	2,547,588	22.2	3,500,556
4-child family	7.3	824,788	7.7	1,214,208
5-child family	2.2	251,370	2.8	440,765
6-child family	0.6	68,706	0.9	147,786
7-child family	0.1	14,700	0.2	36,162
8-child family	0.05	5,360	0.1	20,128
9-child family	0.0	0	0.03	5,067
All	100.0	11,249,634	100.0	15,794,469
Sample size		*14,468*		*19,077*

Notes:

[1] Weighted percentages and weighted numbers. Unweighted sample size.

[2] Percentage/number of dependent children within a single benefit unit.

[3] Percentage/number of children aged under 25 within a single household. Non-dependent children form their own benefit unit.

Source: FRS 2003/04

The research reported here, commissioned by the JRF, has run in parallel with another study of 'The economic position of large families' (Berthoud and Iacovou, 2006), undertaken by the Institute for Social and Economic Research (ISER) at the University of Essex and commissioned by the Department for Work and Pensions. The two reports are to be published at the same time. Although there are inevitably some points of overlap between the two studies, they have been designed to complement each other. The ISER study follows large families through a sequence of processes that affect their economic positions: family formation, employment, income and deprivation. Our study, however, takes a much more direct route in plotting the increased risk of poverty among large families, both in the UK and in an international context. Our focus is on the extent to which tax and benefit policies impact on the risk of poverty for families of various sizes. Readers of either of these reports will probably benefit from reading both.

This report is organised in the following way:

- In the remainder of this chapter we discuss why child poverty in large families is important and why it deserves attention.
- In Chapter 2 we review the issue of poverty in large families in an historical context.
- In Chapter 3 we summarise the current evidence from official sources on child poverty in large families.

- In Chapter 4 we report the results of an analysis of three different data sets designed to explore the characteristics of large families and to test the hypothesis that children in large families are poor independently of other characteristics.
- In Chapter 5 we make some comparisons of child poverty in large families in the UK with other countries and we also assess the extent to which pre-transfer child poverty rates are mitigated by social benefits.
- In Chapter 6 we examine how families of different sizes are treated comparatively.
- In Chapter 7 we explore the costs and effects of a variety of changes in tax and benefit policies designed to benefit large families.
- Finally, in Chapter 8, we provide a conclusion.

Why be concerned with child poverty among large families?

It is not a good thing for our society that any child should be poor. It is not good for the current well-being of the child – their childhood is likely to be constrained. Lack of resources will have an impact on their health, diet, leisure and their capacity to participate in normal childhood activities (for a review of the evidence see Bradshaw and Mayhew, 2005). There is a host of evidence that a poor childhood will lead to poor outcomes in adulthood – lower educational attainment, less good employment outcomes, less happy outcomes in their relationships with partners and in turn their children have a higher risk of poverty as well (Gregg and Machin, 2001; Hobcraft and Kiernan, 2001). This is why child poverty is now at the heart of the domestic social policy agenda, through the commitment to eradicate it.

So no child should be poor. But there are perhaps stronger arguments to be made about a child in a large family being poor. Child poverty generally may be the consequence of parents' unemployment, parents' relationship breakdowns, or their disablement, lack of skills, and so forth. However, although none of these chances can be blamed on a child, poverty in a child in large families (especially if, as we shall see, it is associated with family size per se) is a chance of birth. It therefore falls, perhaps more than other events, under the umbrella of 'luck inegalitarianism' (Anderson, 1999; McLaughlin and Byrne, 2005). It is a particular example of brute luck in the sense that there is no element of choice for the child in their birth order or the size of the family they end up in. Therefore if it is associated with child poverty it is a particular injustice for the child. That is not to deny that many people raised in large families report much joy and fulfilment from the experience, although there is evidence that poverty is not the only disadvantage suffered by children in large families – it also appears to have an impact on educational outcomes.[2]

---

[2] Iacovou (2001) explored the relationship between the number of siblings, birth order and educational outcomes using the National Child Development Study (1958 cohort). She found that having two or more siblings is associated with worse educational outcomes. For family sizes of between three and eight children, each additional sibling is associated with a reduction in test or examination performance. Being an eldest child is associated with an increase in text or examination performance. Children lower down the birth order do worse than those higher up the birth order. However, Iacovou also found that only children perform worse than children from two-child families, even after controlling for a range of parental and school characteristics. This suggests that as well as parental attention, interactions with other children may be important in children's educational development. Similarly, Ermisch and Francesconi (2001) explored the educational attainments of more recent cohorts of British youth (born between 1974 and 1981) using the first seven years (1991-97) of the British Household Panel Study. Those young people with more brothers and sisters, particularly the latter, had lower educational attainments.

However, the main determinant of a child's living standards and quality of life is what their parents earn. There is little rationale for existing differentials in earnings but, with the exception of Japan where large firms pay family allowances, capitalism holds to the principle of equal value for equal work. Need does not come into it. However, in most capitalist economies the state has recognised that it has a role in supporting the substantial financial burdens carried by the few adults who at any one time are raising children.

The extent of responsibility that governments assign themselves, for the financial support of families with children, is reflected in their family policies, which in turn influence their nation's (child) poverty rates.

An historical perspective

The association between poverty and family size was the focus of Eleanor Rathbone's *The disinherited family*, first published in 1924. She recognised that a working-class wage was insufficient to meet the needs of a couple with children and this was one of the main arguments she used in her campaign for family allowances. Beveridge incorporated family allowances in his scheme for social security and family allowances were eventually introduced for the second and subsequent child in 1946. For a time perhaps it was thought that family allowances had solved the problem, because the issue of poverty in large families really only emerged again in the early 1960s. Perhaps the most important study that led to the rediscovery of the problem was by Land (1969). As a pilot for Townsend's (1979) *Poverty in the United Kingdom*, Land conducted a qualitative study of large families containing a sample of 86 families with five or more dependent children living in London. Her study examined several aspects of life in large families including: income and budgeting; housing conditions; task-division within the home; the role of schools and social services; and attitudes towards family planning. She found that the main disadvantages of living in a large family (independent of family income) for children were: overcrowded living conditions, less parental attention, less opportunity to develop their own interests and a disadvantage in the education system. These drawbacks were magnified when poverty was an additional factor, which also introduced health inequalities, social exclusion and stigma from the community. Townsend (1979) in his survey of 2,052 households in the UK found a strong association between relative deprivation and the number of children in the family – 61% of families with four or more children were living in poverty.

HM Treasury's *Child poverty review* (2004, p 6) announced 'a long term aspiration to improve the financial support available to large families'. Long-term implies that it will be achieved by gearing benefit rates towards larger families over a period of years. But how does the tax benefit system treat families of different sizes today? How has this changed over time? What are the implied equivalence scales[3] (see Box 2) in the tax and benefit system and how have these equivalence scales changed over time? These are the questions to be answered in this chapter.

Box 2: Equivalence scales

When we study income poverty by comparing family income with an income threshold, in order to compare like with like, we use an equivalence scale. This scale is used to adjust the income of different families so that, for example, the income of a single person is equivalent to the income of a couple with three children. So, for example, if a childless couple needs £100 per week to reach the poverty threshold then a couple with two children might need £140 per week to reach the same level of living. Equivalence scales are derived in a variety of ways. Originally such scales were influenced by budget standards derived for varying family types. When we undertook the Poverty and Social Exclusion Survey (Gordon et al, 2000) we used such a scale based on the work

continued.../

---

[3] Equivalence scales are a means of adjusting income so that it treats different families equivalently. Tax and benefit systems treat families of different types differently so they have implied equivalence scales.

of the Family Budget Unit. Another approach has been to compare the income levels at which families of different types spend the same proportion of their incomes on necessities (or luxuries). Economists have used more sophisticated econometric analysis of expenditure patterns of different families to derive equivalence scales. In the UK we have been using the McClements scale, named after a government economist who derived it, using these econometric techniques. The Organisation for Economic Co-operation and Development (OECD) developed an equivalence scale from a consensus of national scales. Then, as a result of anxiety that it was too generous to children, it adopted the scale that has become the norm – the modified OECD scale. The government has recently decided to replace the McClements scale with the modified OECD scale – to bring us into line with European practice. Some economists have adopted the square root of the number of people in the household as their equivalence scale on the grounds that it is easy to estimate and close to the modified OECD scale. However, there is very little scientific evidence to support any of these scales.

When tax and benefit systems vary payments for families of different types they have an 'implied' equivalence scale. They are making a judgement of the relative needs of different families. There is considerable room for debate regarding the validity of these judgements about the relative needs of families. For example, the original National Assistance Board scales in 1948 for children were lower as a proportion of the adult's scales than Beveridge had proposed in 1942 (Baldwin and Cooke, 1984), although Beveridge's 1942 proposals were substantially more generous to children than Rowntree's 1935 Human Needs Scale (Field, 1985; Bradshaw and Lynes, 1995).

Equivalence scales are particularly important in a study of income poverty that compares poverty rates in families of different sizes. However, the equivalence scale used tends to determine the results. In this study we have used different scales in different parts of the analysis and sometimes we have compared results obtained using different scales.

On the face of it UK policies are not particularly sensitive to the needs of large families:

- Child Benefit (CB) is paid at a higher rate for the first child in a family.
- The Family Premium in Income Support (IS) effectively results in there being a premium for the first child in a family receiving IS. Beyond that the IS child additions vary only by age and disablement.
- Working Tax Credit is paid at a standard rate regardless of the number of children.
- The Child Support Agency (CSA) formula allows 17% of the income of a non-resident parent for the first child, 20% for the second child and 25% for the third *and subsequent child*.
- Childcare Tax Credit allows 70% of the costs of regulated childcare for *up to two children only*.
- Child Tax Credit (CTC) is a standard amount for each child except that there is a premium for a disabled child. However, the uprating of CTC has benefited large families more because the child rate has been increased in line with earnings while the family element has been frozen.

How have the needs of families of different sizes changed over time?

The first part of the analysis uses a series published by the Department for Work and Pensions (DWP). *The abstract of statistics* produces a time series analysis derived from the DWP's annual Tax benefit model tables of the net income after housing costs (AHC) of a variety of hypothetical family types at various earnings levels (DWP, 2004a, 2004b). From this we have derived implied equivalence scales for families with children. The latest edition of *The abstract of statistics* includes data for each April between 1972 and 2004. In the analysis below we have focused on couples with no children and one, two and three children and selected some years before 1997 and each year since then. This covers the tax benefit treatment of families with earnings. In addition we have used *The abstract of statistics* to compare the incomes of families on IS. In this case the series only goes back to 1988 when IS replaced Supplementary Benefit.

Families in employment

Table 2 presents results for families on average earnings. This is a level of earnings beyond the scope of means-tested benefits except that a fixed rate of CTC is still payable. So the implied equivalence scales are influenced only by that and CB and before 1977 the value of family allowances and child tax allowances. The choice of the comparator or base family makes a difference to the implied equivalence scales obtained and so three separate base families have been chosen. The conventional comparison is with a childless couple = 1.00. We have taken selected years from 1972 to 1997 and then each year under the Labour government. In 1972 a family with three children on average earnings received 15% more than a childless couple. By 1992 that percentage had fallen to only 9% more than a childless couple. This followed a period from 1982 when CB 'withered on the vine' by being uprated by less than movements in the Retail Price Index (RPI) or not uprated at all between April 1987 and April 1991. When CB was eventually uprated in 1991 the government introduced a higher rate for the first child in the family, and that differential was sustained and then eventually increased substantially by the uprating in April 1999, which was 25.8% for the first child and only 3.2% for the second and subsequent children. It can be seen that the result of this was a fall in the relative value of CB for a three-child family compared to a one-child family from 6% in 1992 to only 4% in 2004. Differentials for the average earning families were not helped by the family element of CTC not varying with family size.

So there is evidence here that compared with a one-child couple the implied equivalence scale for large families has deteriorated considerably since 1972. The reasons for this are that CB was relatively less generous to large families than Family Allowances and Child Tax Allowances had been and CB has a premium for the first child in a family.

Table 2: Net income in employment at average earnings (AHC): implied equivalence scales

Selected years	Implied equivalence scales. Childless couple = 1.00			Implied equivalence scale for a couple with three children	
	1 child	2 children	3 children	One-child couple = 1.00	Two-child couple = 1.00
1972	1.02	1.08	1.15	1.12	1.06
1982	1.03	1.08	1.14	1.10	1.05
1992	1.03	1.06	1.09	1.06	1.03
1997	1.03	1.05	1.08	1.05	1.03
1998	1.03	1.05	1.08	1.05	1.03
1999	1.04	1.05	1.09	1.05	1.03
2000	1.04	1.05	1.09	1.05	1.04
2001	1.07	1.08	1.11	1.04	1.03
2002	1.06	1.08	1.11	1.04	1.03
2003	1.09	1.10	1.14	1.04	1.03
2004	1.09	1.10	1.14	1.04	1.03

Source: DWP (2004a)

However, this is based on average earnings and average earnings are a long way above the kind of income level that people in poverty experience. So, in Table 3 we present the same results for families on half average earnings. At this level of earnings the net incomes of families with children are influenced not only by CB but also by in-work benefits – Family Income Supplement, Family Credit, Working Families' Tax Credit (WFTC), Child and Working Tax Credits and Housing and Council Tax Benefits. Overall, the implied equivalence scale is more generous to couples with children – in 1972 a couple with three children received 56% more than a childless couple at half average earnings.

Table 3: Net income in employment at half average earnings (AHC): implied equivalence scales

Selected years	Implied equivalence scales. Childless couple = 1.00			Implied equivalence scale for a couple with three children	
	1 child	2 children	3 children	One-child couple = 1.00	Two-child couple = 1.00
1972	1.14	1.34	1.56	1.36	1.16
1982	1.13	1.32	1.55	1.37	1.17
1992	1.07	1.20	1.44	1.34	1.19
1997	1.12	1.28	1.50	1.35	1.18
1998	1.10	1.24	1.47	1.34	1.18
1999	1.11	1.28	1.50	1.35	1.18
2000	1.36	1.57	1.83	1.35	1.17
2001	1.37	1.58	1.83	1.34	1.16
2002	1.35	1.56	1.80	1.33	1.16
2003	1.34	1.54	1.78	1.33	1.16
2004	1.35	1.57	1.83	1.35	1.16

Source: DWP (2004a)

The story of why the implied equivalence scale changed over this period is complicated:

- The implied equivalence of a three-child family compared with a childless couple fell between 1972 and 1998.
- It recovered in 2000 and 2001 thanks to the introduction of WFTC and compared to a childless couple was higher in 2004 than it was in 1972.
- More important are the relativities compared to a one-child family and here the table shows a remarkably consistent picture. In 1972 a three-child family on half average earnings received 36% more than a one-child family and in 2004 it was 35% more.

Families out of employment

So far we have reviewed the implied equivalence scales in the tax and benefit package for families with children in employment. Now we do the same for families out of employment and on IS (or income-based Jobseeker's Allowance, JSA). It is assumed that all children are less than 16 years old. It can be seen in Table 4 that since 1988 and especially since 1999 there has been a marked improvement in the implied equivalence scale for couples with children over childless couples. This is because the family premium and child scale rates have been uprated faster than the adult scale rates. Since 1999 there has also been an improvement in the implied equivalence of a three-child family over a one-child family. This has been achieved as a result of the scale rates for children being uprated more than the family premium in each year since 1999.

Table 4: Implied equivalence scales for families on social assistance

Selected years	Implied equivalence scales. Childless couple = 1.00			Implied equivalence scale for a couple with three children	
	1 child	2 children	3 children	One-child couple = 1.00	Two-child couple = 1.00
1988	1.33	1.54	1.75	1.16	1.14
1992	1.36	1.58	1.80	1.16	1.14
1997	1.36	1.58	1.80	1.16	1.14
1998	1.36	1.58	1.80	1.16	1.14
1999	1.42	1.67	1.92	1.18	1.15
2000	1.50	1.82	2.15	1.22	1.18
2001	1.55	1.93	2.31	1.24	1.20
2002	1.57	1.97	2.36	1.25	1.20
2003	1.63	2.08	2.53	1.28	1.22
2004	1.67	2.15	2.64	1.29	1.23

Source: DWP (2004a)

So there is evidence here that compared with a childless couple the implied equivalence scale has fallen for large families in employment and on average earnings, and risen for both those in employment on half average earnings and also for those not in employment. However, as we shall see, any real improvements in the scales have had limited success in lifting large families out of poverty. This is partly because benefits are still not high enough to lift low-income families above the poverty threshold and partly because the poverty threshold is derived using a different set of equivalence scales to those implicit in benefit rates.

Table 5 compares some of the conventionally used equivalence scales (see Box 2, p 5) with our implied equivalence scales. The McClements scale currently used in Households Below Average Income (HBAI) to monitor the anti-poverty strategy and the modified OECD scale (that is going to replace it) are relatively more generous to large families than the implied equivalence scale for families on average earnings compared with a childless couple. However, the implied equivalence scales on IS and on half average earnings are more generous than the modified OECD and McClements scales, at least compared with a childless couple. Compared with a one-child family the half average earnings implied equivalence scale is more generous than the actual scale and the implied IS scale less generous than the actual scales.

Table 5: Comparisons of implied equivalence scales and actual equivalence scales

	Equivalence scales. Childless couple = 1.00			Equivalence scale for a couple with three children	
	1 child	2 children	3 children	One–child couple = 1.00	Two–child couple = 1.00
Actual equivalence scales					
OECD	1.29	1.58	1.87	1.44	1.18
Modified OECD	1.20	1.40	1.60	1.33	1.14
McClements BHC	1.20	1.40	1.60	1.33	1.14
Square root of N	1.22	1.41	1.58	1.29	1.12
Implied equivalence scales					
On average earnings 2004	1.09	1.10	1.14	1.04	1.03
On half average earnings 2004	1.35	1.57	1.83	1.35	1.16
On Income Support 2004	1.67	2.15	2.64	1.29	1.23

Source: Own calculation

In summary, for working families on average incomes the implied equivalence for three-child families has deteriorated since the 1970s and 1980s. For low-earning families the picture is less clear and depends to some extent on the actual level of earnings. However, there was an improvement in the implied equivalence for families with children after 2000 but it did not favour three-child families.

Child poverty in large families

Large families are in decline (see Box 3) but children in large families still have a higher risk of poverty. We shall be investigating why this is in more detail later but here we present the headline figures and trends. It can be seen in Table 6 that in 2004/05 (the latest available data from the Family Resources Survey), 10% of dependent children lived in a family containing four or more children in the UK (DWP, 2005). If we take the official headline poverty threshold of below 60% of equivalent contemporary median before housing costs 41% of those children were poor. After housing costs 50% were poor. The child poverty rate in one-child families was 15% before housing costs and 23% after housing costs.

Table 6: Child poverty rates by family size 2004/05

	Equivalent income <50% median	Equivalent income <60% median	Equivalent income <70% median	All
BHC				
1 child	8	15	23	25
2 children	9	16	27	45
3 children	11	22	37	20
4+ children	24	41	62	10
AHC				
1 child	16	23	29	25
2 children	15	23	32	45
3 children	17	30	42	20
4+ children	31	50	65	10

Source: DWP (2006), Table 4.7

Box 3: Trends in the prevalence of large families

Trends in fertility have been changing the family size structure of Britain. Large families have been in decline. Figure 1 shows that over the last 50 years there has been very little reduction in the proportion of women having one or two children. However, there has been a sharp decrease in the proportion having three and in particular four or more children. As a result, the average completed family size is getting smaller, falling from 2.19 in the 1945 cohort to 1.75 in the 1990 cohort. Rates of childlessness among women increased dramatically towards the end of the 20th century. Only 9% of the 1945 cohort of women was childless compared with 20% of those born in 1965. While some women are voluntarily childless, others may be unable to have children due to fertility problems. The postponement of motherhood to later in life can lead to difficulties in conceiving (ONS, 2003). It is estimated that as many as 25% of the present cohorts of fecund women will remain childless.

continued.../

Figure 1: Percentage of children by women's year of birth (projections from 1965), England and Wales

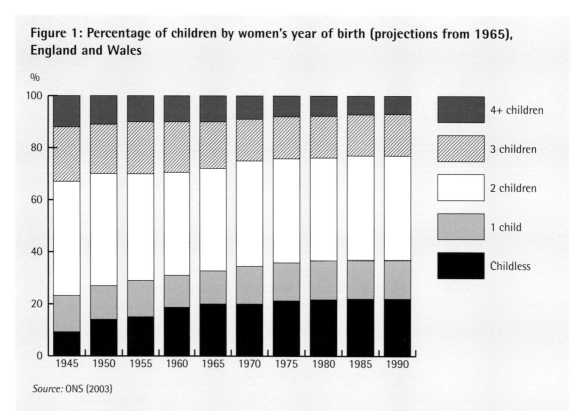

Source: ONS (2003)

Table 7 shows the change in the composition of family types containing children in Britain. Over the last 30 years there has been a reduction in the number of children living in large (3+) couple families and an increase in the number living in lone-parent families of all sizes and types (including large ones).

Table 7: Percentage of children living in different family types (Britain)

	1972	1981	1992	2001	2004
Couple families					
1 child	16	18	18	17	17
2 children	35	41	39	38	37
3+ children	41	29	27	25	23
Lone-mother families					
1 child	2	3	4	6	7
2 children	2	4	5	7	9
3+ children	2	3	4	5	6
Lone-father families					
1 child	–	1	1	1	1
2+ children	1	1	1	1	1
All children	*100*	*100*	*100*	*100*	*100*

Source: National Statistics (2005), Table 2.4

Original sources: General Household Survey, Census, Labour Force Survey

So children in large families have a much higher risk of poverty than children in small families. However, it can be seen in Figure 2 (before housing costs, BHC) and Figure 3 (after housing costs, AHC) that the poverty of children in 3-child and 4+ child families has been falling, falling faster than for children in small families. We think that this might be explained by two factors: improvements in employment rates of couples with large numbers of children after 1998/99 (although Berthoud and Iacovou [2006] suggest that this did not happen); and the introduction of Working Families' Tax Credit (WFTC), which began to improve in-work incomes from October 2000.

Figure 2: Child poverty (% living in households with <60% of contemporary median household income, BHC) rate by number of children in the family

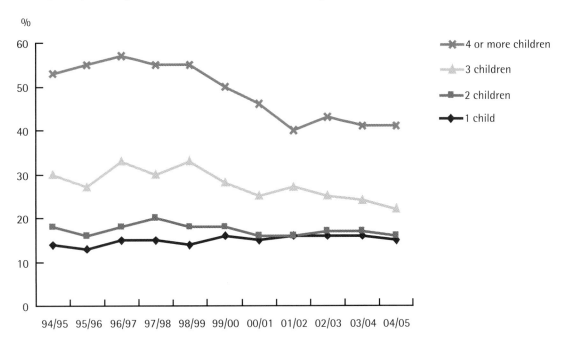

Source: DWP (2006), Table E4.1

Figure 3: Child poverty (% living in households with <60% of contemporary median household income, AHC) rate by number of children in the family

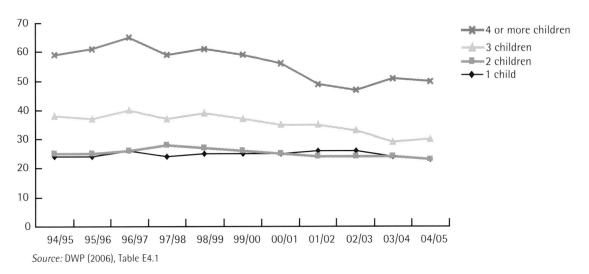

Source: DWP (2006), Table E4.1

In 2004/05 children in families with three or more children made up 42% of the children in poverty (60% median threshold AHC). However, Figure 4 shows that the proportion is lower than it was in 1999/2000. Nevertheless, if the government is going to achieve its target to eradicate child poverty, more attention is going to have to be paid to large families.

Figure 4: Composition of children in poverty by family size, AHC (%)

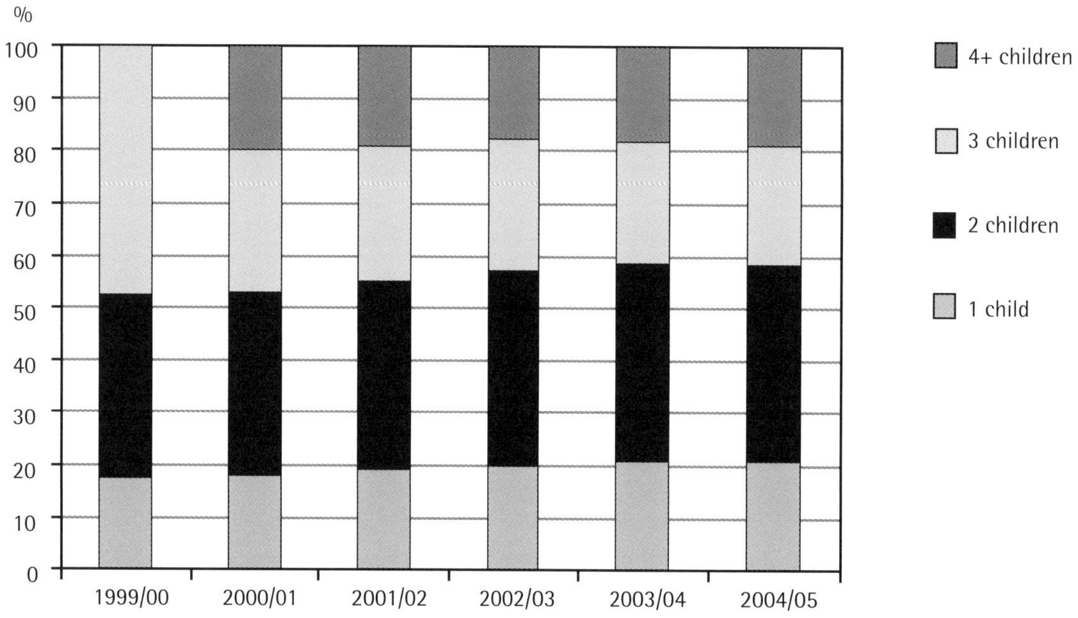

Source: DWP (2006), Table 6.1

The characteristics of poor children in large families

This chapter uses three large data sets to explore the characteristics of large families. We establish that the number of children is a factor associated with child poverty independently of other characteristics of the family. This analysis builds on earlier research.

Berthoud and Ford (1996) and Ford (1997) used four surveys (Poor Britain, 1983; Poverty in London, 1986; Credit and Debt, 1989; Low Income Families, 1991) to examine the living standards of families. Five indicators were used to represent living standards: diet, clothing, housing, social participation and indebtedness. A single indicator was derived from the five indicators. There was a strong negative association between the standard of living indicator and the number of children in the household. The more children, the lower the standard of living. However, they found that ownership of consumer durables was an indicator that was positively associated with the number of children in the family – large families with children were more likely to possess durables than others on the same income. Among the possible reasons for this were that the same durable will be of more use for a large family; families with more children are more likely to have durables because they are longer established; and Social Fund payments may make it easier for some of the lowest-income families with children to possess durables.

Gordon et al (2000) in the Poverty and Social Exclusion (PSE) Survey of Britain found there was no significant difference in the deprivation of children with no siblings and with one sibling using a threshold based on the lack of socially perceived necessities (items and activities that more than half the population judged to be necessities. However, the deprivation levels of children in households with three or more children increased dramatically (86% of 4+ child families lacked one or more item compared to 11% of one-child families).

The increased vulnerability of large families to poverty was confirmed by the study carried out by Adelman et al (2003). They found that children experiencing persistent (lasting over three years) and severe poverty (that is, poor on all three poverty measures used by the study) were more likely to come from large families (59% of children who experienced persistent and severe poverty came from a family containing three or more children, while only 24% of children who were classed as 'not poor' belonged to a large family).

In multivariate analysis of the Families and Children Study (FaCS) and using a measure of deprivation, a study by Berthoud et al (2004) indicated sharply increasing levels of deprivation in families as the number of children in the family increased. Willitts and Swales (2003) also used the FaCS 2001) to examine the characteristics of families with three or more dependent children. Large families compared to small families were more likely to:

- have older parents;
- have the youngest child under five years of age;
- be from a Pakistani, Indian or Bangladeshi background;
- have lower levels of employment;
- have higher levels of hardship both in and out of work;
- receive social security benefits.

Family size remained important in predicting hardship even when a range of other factors were controlled for.

Family Resources Survey

The Family Resources Survey (FRS) is an annual survey that collects information on the incomes and circumstances of 25,000 private households in the UK and our analysis uses the last available wave for 2003/04. We selected households containing single benefit units – that is, households headed by a single person or a couple who is economically active (that is, employed and/or entitled to benefits) and where all other members of the household are dependent children – and the unit of analysis is the child. The FRS contains information on 16,396 individual children. However, a 'benefit unit grossing factor' is used in order to make the results of the analyses representative of the population of the UK. We define 'income poverty' as below 60% of the median before housing costs (BHC) and after housing costs (AHC). The equivalence scale used is, except where stated, the McClements scale (see Box 2, p 6).

First, we explore in simple cross-tabulations how family size varies with some of the other characteristics of the families. In Table 8 we explore the relationship between the number of children and employment. In couple families both parents are most likely to be employed when they have two children and lone parents are most likely to be employed when they have one child. Children of workless parents are four times more likely to be in a large family than a one-child family and children in a workless lone-parent family are four times more likely to be in a large family than children with a working lone parent. Large families are associated with worklessness.

Table 8: Proportion of children in household by parental employment status*

Employment status	Family with 1 child	Family with 2 children	Family with 3 children	Family with 4+ children
2 parents, both working	41.9	49.3	43.1	24.8
2 parents, one working	21.2	25.2	28.1	38.0
2 parents, neither working	4.6	4.3	6.8	16.1
Lone parent working	17.6	10.4	8.3	4.3
Lone parent not working	14.7	10.7	13.7	16.8
All	*100.0*	*100.0*	*100.0*	*100.0*
Sample size	*2,914*	*6,484*	*3,327*	*1,604*

Note:* p < 0.001 Weighted percentages, unweighted sample sizes.

Source: Own analysis of the FRS 2003/04

Table 9 shows that there are fewer white ethnic group children in families with 4+ children than other sized families, and that Pakistani or Bangladeshi, Black and Other (including Chinese) children are more likely to be living in 4+ child families. Families from an Indian ethnic background have similar proportions of children in small and large families.

Table 9: Proportion of children in household by ethnicity of household head*

Ethnic group	Family with 1 child	Family with 2 children	Family with 3 children	Family with 4+ children
White	90.3	92.2	89.1	79.9
Mixed	1.2	0.7	0.7	1.8
Indian	1.7	2.1	1.9	1.8
Pakistani or Bangladeshi	1.4	0.9	2.7	9.6
Black Caribbean or Black African	3.6	2.3	3.7	4.2
Other	1.9	1.9	1.9	2.7
All	*100.0*	*100.0*	*100.0*	*100.0*
Sample size	*2,909*	*6,474*	*3,318*	*1,600*

Note: *p < 0.001 Weighted percentages, unweighted sample sizes.
Source: Own analysis of the FRS 2003/04

Table 10 shows, as might be expected, that children of young mothers tend to live in smaller families but so do children of the 45 and over age group – presumably as a result of children leaving home.

Table 10: Proportion of children in household by mother's age*

Age	Family with 1 child	Family with 2 children	Family with 3 children	Family with 4+ children
16-24	12.7	4.5	1.5	1.4
25-34	34.9	31.8	30.5	39.8
35-44	34.1	52.8	59.5	52.7
45 and over	18.3	10.9	8.5	6.2
All	*100.0*	*100.0*	*100.0*	*100.0*
Sample size	*2,876*	*6,420*	*3,291*	*1,570*

Note: *p < 0.001 Weighted percentages, unweighted sample sizes.
Source: Own analysis of the FRS 2003/04

Table 11, however, shows that children of mothers who have their first child when they are aged under 20 are much more likely to be living in large families than one-child families. This suggests that mothers who start their child bearing younger tend to have more children.

Table 11: Proportion of children in household by mother's age at first birth*

Age	Family with 1 child	Family with 2 children	Family with 3 children	Family with 4+ children
14-19	8.4	7.8	13.1	26.1
20-24	19.7	25.1	34.5	45.3
25-29	27.4	37.3	34.7	19.2
30-34	26.8	23.1	15.2	8.0
35-39	15.8	6.4	2.4	1.1
40 and over	2.0	0.4	0.2	0.2
All	*100.0*	*100.0*	*100.0*	*100.0*
Sample size	*2,833*	*6,354*	*3,252*	*1,520*

Note: *p < 0.001 Weighted percentages, unweighted sample sizes.

Source: Own analysis of the FRS 2003/04

Table 12 shows that family size is also related to mothers' educational level, with a higher proportion of children in 4+ child families having a mother who left school at 16 or under.

Table 12: Proportion of children in household by age at which mother left full-time education*

Age	Family with 1 child	Family with 2 children	Family with 3 children	Family with 4+ children
16 or under	51.3	49.8	52.9	60.6
17-18	25.3	26.6	25.4	24.9
Over 18	23.4	23.6	21.7	14.5
All	*100.0*	*100.0*	*100.0*	*100.0*
Sample size	*2,828*	*6,344*	*3,246*	*1,532*

Note: *p < 0.001 Weighted percentages, unweighted sample sizes.

Source: Own analysis of the FRS 2003/04

Table 13 shows that children in families in Northern Ireland and London are more likely to live in large families.

Table 13: Proportion of children in household by region/nation*

Region	Family with 1 child	Family with 2 children	Family with 3 children	Family with 4+ children	All	*Sample size*
London	23.5	40.8	22.5	13.2	100	1,338
England**	20.4	46.5	23.2	9.9	100	9,327
Wales	22.0	48.7	17.4	12.0	100	569
Scotland	24.6	47.8	20.4	7.2	100	2,063
N. Ireland	21.4	39.0	23.3	16.3	100	1,171

Notes: *p < 0.001 Weighted percentages, unweighted sample sizes. **England excluding London.

Source: Own analysis of the FRS 2003/04

Table 14 shows that children in families with the youngest child under five years of age are also more likely to be living in large families.

Table 14: Proportion of children in household by age of youngest child*

Age	Family with 1 child	Family with 2 children	Family with 3 children	Family with 4+ children
4 and under	42.7	40.3	44.1	58.4
5-10	23.6	36.7	44.9	36.2
11-15	22.0	22.0	10.7	5.4
16-19	11.6	1.1	0.3	0.0
All	*100.0*	*100.0*	*100.0*	*100.0*
Sample size	*2,979*	*6,536*	*3,339*	*1,614*

Notes: *p < 0.001 *weighted percentages, unweighted sample sizes. **England excluding London.

Source: Own analysis of the FRS 2003/04

Table 15 assesses the sensitivity of the child poverty rate by family size to a variety of equivalence scales (see Box 1, p 1). This analysis is based on the 60% of median income threshold for families with children so it is not comparable with the child poverty rates in Table 6. The PSE scale, which is most generous to children (and lone parents), produces the highest child poverty rates in large families. The modified Organisation for Economic Co-operation and Development (OECD) scale produces slightly higher overall child poverty rates than the Households Below Average Income (HBAI) (McClement's) scale but not for children in large families. This analysis shows that the child poverty rates in families of different sizes are sensitive to the equivalence scale used.

This table also gives the size of the poverty gap (the average difference between income and the poverty threshold). In couple families it increases with the number of children. For lone parents the poverty gap is widest for a lone parent with two children.

Table 15: Child poverty rate and poverty gaps for different family types using a variety of equivalence scales (%)*

	BHC				AHC				Sample size	BHC HBAI poverty gap**
	HBAI	PSE	OECD	MOD OECD	HBAI	PSE	OECD	MOD OECD	*Numbers*	Mean % household income
Two parents plus 1 child	8.7	4.9	9.6	9.9	12.9	8.4	13.3	13.7	*1,995*	26.0
Two parents plus 2 children	8.5	8.0	9.5	8.9	12.0	11.6	13.5	12.2	*5,038*	29.5
Two parents plus 3 children	11.6	17.0	14.2	11.8	15.1	19.9	17.6	14.5	*2,562*	8.8
Two parents plus 4+ children	26.3	49.6	32.8	24.0	31.9	49.4	37.4	29.7	*1,213*	23.4
Lone parent plus 1 child	12.9	11.3	13.7	22.3	38.9	43.4	45.0	48.4	*984*	23.6
Lone parent plus 2 children	17.9	42.6	23.0	22.8	35.5	54.6	50.0	49.9	*1,498*	58.6
Lone parent plus 3 children	25.2	57.9	33.7	28.9	39.6	62.0	50.9	48.8	*777*	20.5
Lone parent plus 4+ children	22.9	82.8	42.3	21.1	42.6	83.7	73.2	44.1	*401*	8.8
Total	12.9	20.2	15.7	14.3	20.4	26.0	24.9	22.8	*14,468*	26.4

Notes:

*Weighted percentages, Unweighted sample sizes.

**Based on BHC HBAI equivalent income.

We have seen that family size is associated with child poverty. However, we have also seen in the cross-tabulations that many other socioeconomic factors are associated with family size. Many of them are also associated with poverty. Does family size have an association with poverty independently of these other factors?

Table 16 shows, as we would expect from the analysis above, that before controlling for other factors the odds of a child being poor are higher in large families, in lone-parent families, in families with not all parents working, for children with young first-time mothers, in families with a child aged four and under, for some ethnic groups, where mothers left school at aged 16 or under, in London and in families with a disabled member.

Table 16: Odds of *child* experiencing poverty (60% below median BHC equivalised income [HBAI] measure)

	Not controlling for other factors	Controlling for all other factors
Family size		
1-child family	1.00	1.00
2-child family	1.05***	1.21***
3-child family	1.53***	1.53***
4-child family	2.48***	1.67***
5+ child family	4.91***	3.68***
Family type		
Couple with children	1.00	1.00
Lone parent with children	1.81***	0.44***
Number of earners in household		
Two earners	1.00	1.00
One earner	4.02***	4.70***
No earners	13.53***	25.17***
Mother's age at first birth		
Under 21	1.00	1.00
21-27	0.66***	1.12***
28 and over	0.36***	0.92***
Age of youngest child		
4 and under	1.00	1.00
5-10	1.01***	1.60***
11-15	1.08***	2.41***
16-19	0.81***	2.53***
Ethnicity of head of household		
White	1.00	1.00
Mixed	2.00***	1.69***
Indian	2.84***	3.49***
Pakistani or Bangladeshi	8.28***	4.81***
Black Caribbean or Black African	2.54***	2.44***
Other	3.26***	5.07***
Mother's age when leaving full-time education		
16 or under	1.00	1.00
16-18	0.47***	0.57***
Over 18	0.56***	0.74***
UK region/nation		
London	1.00	1.00
England	0.64***	1.30***
Wales	0.53***	1.10***
Scotland	0.71***	1.62***
Northern Ireland	0.74***	1.73***
Whether there is anyone disabled in the household		
None	1.00	1.00
One or more	1.27***	0.54***

Notes: ***$p < 0.001$, **$p < 0.01$, *$p < 0.05$

Source: Own analysis of FRS 2003/04

After controlling for all factors simultaneously family size still remains a strong predictor of child poverty. A child in a 5+ child family is almost four times more likely to be poor than a child in a one-child family. Having controlled for other factors the odds ratios of a child being poor are lower for 4 and 5+ child families but still every extra child in the family increases the odds of being poor. There are changes in the odds of some of the other groups after controlling for other factors (for example, children in lone-parent families are less likely to be in poverty having controlled for other factors) but the family size effect remains strong. So we can conclude that there is an independent influence of family size – child poverty in large families cannot be explained away by the fact that parents in large families are less likely to be employed or more likely to be of Pakistani or Bangladeshi background or any of the other characteristics.

Millennium Cohort Study

The Millennium Cohort Study (MCS) (or Child of the New Century) is a new national longitudinal birth cohort study that was launched in 2000 to mark the new millennium. The first wave of the MCS contains a child population aged nine months (born between September 2000 and January 2002), living in the UK and eligible to receive Child Benefit (CB). The children are being followed up at age three (at the time of writing) and there are plans and funding in place to follow them up again at age five when they will be in school and then at seven years old. The final sample size contains 18,553 families and after allowance for 246 twin and 10 triplet births, the number of babies included in the data set amounts to 18,819. The vast majority of respondents were mothers. The MCS is stratified to over-represent areas with high proportions of minority ethnic groups in England, residents of areas with high child poverty and residents of Scotland, Wales and Northern Ireland. It is therefore an extremely useful and up-to-date vehicle for studying child and family poverty (Bradshaw et al, 2005; Mayhew and Bradshaw, 2005). Income poverty is defined as having a net equivalent household income below 60% of the national median. For the calculation of equivalent income we used the McClements equivalence scale.

We have not undertaken the same type of cross-tabulations with the MCS as with the FRS but have gone directly to the regression analyses of the odds of a baby being poor in the first sweep at about nine months. In Table 17 it can be seen that before controlling for other factors the odds of a child being poor are associated with the number of siblings, marital status, number of earners, mother's age at first birth, mother's ethnicity, mother's educational qualifications, region and whether the mother is disabled.

After controlling for these factors we find again that the number of children in the family is independently associated with higher odds of a child being poor. A baby with 3+ siblings has more than four times the odds of an only child being born poor.

Table 17: Odds of baby being income poor

	Not controlling for other factors	Controlling for all other factors
Number of siblings of baby		
Only child	1.00	1.00
1 sibling	1.12***	1.62***
2 siblings	2.15***	2.80***
3+ siblings	5.15***	4.10***
Family type		
Married natural parents	1.00	1.00
Cohabiting natural parents	2.37***	1.92***
Lone parent	21.29***	2.69***
Number of earners		
2 earners	1.00	1.00
1 earner	6.50***	3.95***
0 earners	166.01***	51.13***
Mother's age at first birth		
Under 21	1.00	1.00
21-27	0.23***	0.59***
28 and over	0.06***	0.32***
Mother's ethnicity		
White	1.00	1.00
Mixed	2.68***	1.57 NS
Indian	1.14***	2.59**
Pakistani or Bangladeshi	5.85***	6.06***
Black or Black British	2.77***	2.62***
Other	1.30***	2.52**
Mother's highest qualification		
None on the list shown	1.00	1.00
NVQ Level 1	0.46***	1.19 NS
NVQ Level 2	0.20***	0.69**
NVQ Level 3	0.14***	0.62***
NVQ Level 4	0.05***	0.37***
NVQ Level 5	0.02***	0.21***
UK region/nation		
London	1.00	1.00
England	1.01 NS	1.43 NS
Wales	1.34**	1.97**
Scotland	1.11 NS	2.09***
Northern Ireland	1.38**	2.96***
Whether mother is disabled		
No	1.00	1.00
Yes	1.30***	1.09 NS

Notes: ***p < 0.001, **p < 0.01, *p < 0.05, NS = not significant.

Source: Own analysis of the MCS 2001

Families and Children Study

The Families and Children Study (FaCS) is a panel survey of families with children. We repeated the previous analysis using the FaCS. We used two measures: income poverty is assessed using equivalent household income before housing costs; material deprivation is measured using the Policy Studies Institute (PSI) 'hardship index' (Vegeris and Perry, 2003). The child is again the unit of analysis.[4]

Table 18 shows the logistic regression results of the odds of a child living in a household with an income below 60% of the median equivalent income BHC (OECD Modified Scale).

Before controlling for other factors the odds of a child living in a household with a low income were higher for:

- large families;
- lone-parent families;
- families from Pakistani/Bangladeshi or Black ethnic backgrounds;
- families where the mother has no educational qualifications;
- families where the main respondent has a long-term illness or disability;
- families who live in social rented accommodation or have other non-specified tenure arrangements;
- families where the respondent had a change in relationship status since joining the survey, either from lone parent to couple or vice versa.

The odds of a child living in a low-income household were reduced if:

- the mother's current age was 25 years or older;
- the youngest child in the family was aged five years or older.

Controlling for variations in various family characteristics increases the odds of a child in a large family being poor. All things being equal (for example, the mother's age and qualifications, age of youngest child, ethnic background, and so on) living in a 4+ child family results in a child's chances of being poor being more than doubled.

We now explore the odds of being in poverty using the PSI hardship index. The index measures a number of material dimensions. The nine indicators in the index are:

- reports two or more problems with quality of accommodation and cannot afford to repair (if owner);
- lives in overcrowded accommodation;
- cannot afford to keep home warm;
- worries about money almost all the time and runs out of money most weeks;
- has no bank account and has two or more problem debts;
- lacks food items;

---

[4] The analysis is conducted on a sub-sample of the FaCS data for wave six (2004), which includes families where all the children are dependent (aged 16 years or less or aged 17-18 years and in full-time education) natural children of the family (including adopted) or stepchildren (11,718 cases). Thus, families with at least one non-dependent child are excluded from the data set, as are individual children whose relationship to the respondent is a foster child, or a grandchild or unrelated child. However, in the construction of the family size variable, this does count all the children in the family regardless of their relationship to the main respondent and therefore it includes stepchildren, foster children, grandchildren and unrelated children living in the household (but not non-dependent children).

- lacks clothing items;
- lacks consumer durables;
- lacks social/leisure activities.

The index is normally collapsed into three simple categories:

- no hardship (no indicators) (68%);
- moderate hardship (one or two indicators) (23%);
- severe hardship (three to nine indicators) (8%).

In Table 19 children were considered to be in hardship if they had at least three indicators in the nine-point index (8% fell into this category).

Having controlled for other factors there is a significant association between hardship and having three, four or more children in the family. The odds of a child in a four-child family living in hardship is 2.89 times that of a child in a one-child family.

Table 20 shows the results of a logistic regression when families experience both hardship and low income *in combination*. Disadvantage here is defined as a child living in a family that experienced two or more incidences of hardship as measured by the PSI nine-point index *and* having a household income below 60% of the median. Overall, only 9% of children experienced a combination of both hardship and low income.

Table 18: Odds of child living in a low-income household (<60% equivalent income BHC, OECD Modified Scale)

Child's family characteristics	Not controlling for other factors	Controlling for all other factors
Family size		
1-child family	1.00	1.00
2-child family	0.63 ***	0.94 NS
3-child family	1.15 *	1.59 ***
4+ child family	2.06 ***	2.33 ***
Mother's current age		
16-24	1.00	1.00
25-34	0.25 ***	0.33 ***
35-44	0.20 ***	0.40 ***
45+	0.21 ***	0.47 ***
Age of youngest child in family		
4 and under	1.00	1.00
5-10	0.59 ***	0.68 ***
11 and over	0.76 ***	1.17 NS
Family type		
Couple with children	1.00	1.00
Lone parent with children *(value code 1)*	3.81 ***	2.47 ***
Ethnicity of respondent[1]		
White or White British	1.00	1.00
Mixed	1.55 NS	0.96 NS
Indian or other Asian	1.38 NS	2.52 ***
Pakistani or Bangladeshi	4.71 ***	4.56 ***
Black or Black British	3.37 ***	1.82 ***
Chinese or other ethnic group	1.55 *	1.70 *
Mother's highest educational qualification		
First or higher degree	1.00	1.00
A levels	1.79 ***	1.47 **
GCSE	3.23 ***	1.97 ***
Other	2.82 ***	1.90 **
No qualifications	7.46 ***	2.67 ***
Respondent reports long-term illness/disability[2]		
No	1.00	1.00
Yes *(value code 1)*	1.39 ***	1.07 NS
Tenure		
Owned/mortgaged	1.00	1.00
Social tenant	6.19 ***	2.90 ***
Private tenant	2.86 ***	1.67 ***
Other arrangement	7.21 ***	5.58 ***
Respondent relationship status changed since joined survey[3]		
No	1.00	1.00
Yes *(value code 1)*	1.33 ***	1.08 NS

Notes:

***p < 0.001, **p < 0.01, *p < 0.05, NS = not significant

[1] Respondent is usually the mother.

[2] Whether a sick/disabled child lived in household was not significant.

[3] Changed from lone parent to couple or vice versa.

Source: Own analysis of the FaCS

Table 19: Odds of a child experiencing relative hardship using two measures of hardship

Child's family characteristics	Hardship = at least three incidences from the nine point PSI Index	
	Not controlling for other factors	Controlling for all other factors
Family size		
1-child family	1.00	1.00
2-child family	0.69***	1.02 NS
3-child family	1.32**	1.71***
4+ child family	2.68***	2.89***
Mother's current age		
16-24	1.00	1.00
25-34	0.37***	0.56***
35-44	0.20***	0.52***
45+	0.14***	0.50**
Age of youngest child in family		
4 and under	1.00	1.00
5-10	0.64***	0.77**
11 years and over	0.39***	0.65***
Family type		
Couple with children	1.00	1.00
Lone parent with children *(value code 1)*	6.11***	3.38***
Ethnicity of respondent[1]		
White or White British	1.00	1.00
Mixed	3.28***	2.58***
Indian or other Asian	1.29 NS	2.48**
Pakistani or Bangladeshi	1.15 NS	1.12 NS
Black or Black British	3.59***	1.65**
Chinese or other ethnic group	1.21 NS	1.67 NS
Mother's highest educational qualifications		
First or higher degree	1.00	1.00
A levels	3.77***	2.59***
GCSE	10.74***	4.56***
Other	4.58***	1.99*
No qualifications	24.14***	6.14***
Main respondent reports long-term illness/disability[2]		
No	1.00	1.00
Yes *(value code 1)*	2.11***	1.86***
Tenure		
Owned/mortgaged	1.00	1.00
Social tenant	11.42***	3.63***
Private tenant	8.46***	3.38***
Other arrangement	4.19***	2.07**
Respondent relationship status changed since joined survey[3]		
No	1.00	1.00
Yes	1.75***	1.38***

Notes:

***p < 0.001, **p < 0.01, *p < 0.05, NS = not significant

[1] Respondent is usually the mother.

[2] Whether a sick/disabled child lived in household was not significant.

[3] Changed from lone parent to couple or vice versa.

Source: Own analysis of FaCS

Table 20: Odds of a child experiencing relative hardship (hardship = at least two incidences from the nine-point PSI Index) combined with low income (<60% equivalent income BHC, OECD Modified Scale)

	Not controlling for other factors	Controlling for all other factors
Family size		
1-child family	1.00	1.00
2-child family	0.66***	1.29 NS
3-child family	1.36**	2.17***
4+ child family	4.21***	7.97***
Mother's current age		
16-24	1.00	1.00
25-34	0.17***	0.20***
35-44	0.11***	0.28***
45+	0.08***	0.31***
Age of youngest child in family		
4 and under	1.00	1.00
5-10	0.47***	0.59***
11 years and over	0.36***	0.61**
Family type		
Couple with children	1.00	1.00
Lone parent with children *(value code 1)*	7.35***	6.25***
Ethnicity of respondent[1]		
White or White British	1.00	1.00
Mixed	3.85***	3.66**
Indian or other Asian	1.38 NS	6.02***
Pakistani or Bangladeshi	5.83***	5.24***
Black or Black British	4.62***	1.75*
Chinese or other ethnic group	1.23 NS	1.79 NS
Mother's highest educational qualifications		
First or higher degree	1.00	1.00
A levels	4.30***	2.61**
GCSE	14.34***	6.94***
Other	4.80**	2.79*
No qualifications	45.26***	11.88***
Main respondent reports long-term illness/disability[2]		
No	1.00	1.00
Yes *(value code 1)*	2.12***	1.91***
Tenure		
Owned/mortgaged	1.00	1.00
Social tenant	17.17***	4.61***
Private tenant	6.65***	2.38***
Other arrangement	8.67***	4.62***
Respondent relationship status changed since joined survey[3]		
No	1.00	1.00
Yes	1.60***	1.31*

Notes:

***p < 0.001, **p < 0.01, *p < 0.05, NS = not significant

[1] Respondent is usually the mother.

[2] Whether a sick/disabled child lived in household was not significant.

[3] Changed from lone parent to couple or vice versa.

Source: Own analysis of FaCS

It can be seen that after controlling for other factors the odds of a child in a four-child family experiencing hardship and low income was nearly eight times the odds for a child in a one-child family.

In all three of the data sets that we have examined, children in large families are more likely to be poor and this remains true even after controlling for other characteristics of families associated with child poverty. In Table 21 we summarise the odds ratios from the regressions which control for the other characteristics of the sample. They vary between the surveys and measures and in the FaCS there is no difference between the odds for a one- and a two-child family but for all the sources there are significantly higher odds for three- and four-child families.

Table 21: Summary of the odds ratios on family size

Family size	FRS	MCS	FaCS (income poverty)	FaCS (deprivation)	FaCS (income and deprivation)
1-child family	1.00	1.00	1.00	1.00	1.00
2-child family	1.21***	1.62***	0.94 NS	1.02 NS	1.29 NS
3-child family	1.53***	2.80***	1.59***	1.71***	2.17***
4+ child family	1.67***	4.10***	2.33***	2.89***	7.97***
5+ child family	3.68***				

Note: ***p < 0.001, **p < 0.01, *p < 0.05, NS = not significant.

5

International comparisons

This chapter provides a comparative perspective on the prevalence of child poverty and especially how the risks of child poverty vary with the number of children in the family. The objective of the analysis is to evaluate whether the UK has a particular problem in respect of child poverty in large families and to assess whether this is associated with the tax and benefit system.

Poverty in large families has been the focus of earlier comparative research. Redmond (2000) examined the relationship between policy, poverty and household size across seven countries (Canada, Australia, the US, Norway, Sweden, Finland and France) using the Luxembourg Income Study (LIS). He found that there was an association between welfare state provision (measured as direct cash benefits paid in respect of children) and overall levels of child poverty. Cantillon and Van den Bosch (2002) also used LIS data and found that the poverty rate among families with three or more children was equally high as that among single-parent families in Belgium, Spain, Finland (although at a comparatively low level), Italy and the UK. The poverty risk of large families generally exceeded that of childless non-aged families, except in the Nordic Countries and the Netherlands. Layte and Fouarge (2004) and Whelan et al (2004) examined the impact of various socioeconomic factors on cross-national differences in deprivation using the European Community Household Panel (ECHP) survey. Logistic regression showed that having a larger number of children (3+) tended to lead to higher levels of deprivation across all countries, but the effect is rather small when compared to other variables (such as long-term unemployment, being a young single person (aged 17-24), or lone parenthood). The negative effect of having a large family was strongest in Italy, Portugal and the UK (followed by Germany and Ireland).

We explore child poverty in large families using both the ECHP and the LIS.

The European Community Household Panel survey

The ECHP is an annual sample survey of households in the EU15 countries. It began in 1994 and the latest and last wave is the 2001 wave, which is used for this analysis. The ECHP is being replaced by the Survey of Income and Living Conditions (SILC) but not all EU25 countries will be included in SILC until 2007.

We define large families as families with three or more children. The child poverty rate is the proportion of children living in households with equivalent income below 60% of the median. The equivalence scale used in this analysis is the traditional Organisation for Economic Co-operation and Development (OECD) equivalence scale (1.0 for the first adult, 0.7 for the second adult, 0.5 per child). The measure used is before housing costs (BHC) because there are reasons to be anxious about the comparability of the housing costs questions in the ECHP.[5] In the ECHP the income data is for the year before the survey so the 2001 survey collects income data for 2000.

---

[5] Housing costs in the Nordic and some other countries include expenditure on domestic fuel while they do not in other countries.

Figure 5 shows that in most countries the risk of child poverty increases with each additional child, although this is not the case for Denmark, Belgium and Finland. However, with the exception of Denmark the risks of child poverty are higher in 3+ child families in all countries. In the UK the risk of child poverty is 15% in a one-child family and 45% in a 3+ child family.

Figure 5: Income child poverty rates (% children in households with equivalent income <60% of the median, BHC) by number of children

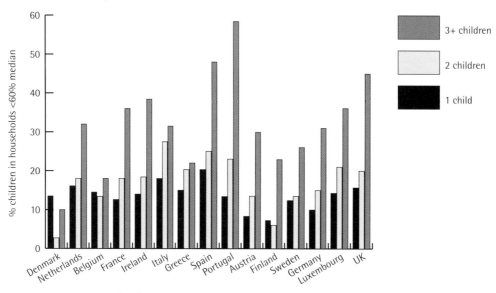

Source: Own analysis of ECHP (2001)

Figure 6 compares the relative risk of child poverty by the number of children, with the overall child poverty rate set to 1.0. Again, in all countries the relative risk for large families is higher than for all families. In Denmark one-child families are at a higher risk of poverty than large families and Belgium has very little variation in the child poverty rate by the number of children. The highest relative risk in 3+ child families is in Greece, Austria and Portugal. The UK pattern is very similar to France (as so often), with the relative risk 60% higher in three-child families.

Figure 6: Relative risk of child poverty (% children in households with equivalent income <60% of the median, BHC). All children = 1.00

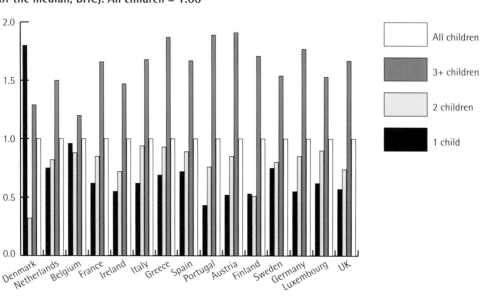

Source: Own analysis of ECHP (2001)

In Figure 7 we explore the effectiveness of the transfer system in each country. This is done by taking the pre-transfer child poverty rate and estimating the percentage reduction in child poverty achieved by cash benefits (tax benefits are not included). It can be seen that the UK comes fourth highest for the child poverty reduction in one-child families; however, it comes eighth in the league table for 3+ child families. While some countries' benefit systems are broadly equitable in their poverty reduction between families of different sizes, the UK (and Ireland and Italy) have a big gap in the child poverty reduction achieved between one-child families and 3+ child families.

This analysis has demonstrated that the risk of child poverty in almost all countries is much higher in large families than small families. The UK relative risk of child poverty in large families is comparatively high and the benefit system is one of the least effective in reducing pre-transfer child poverty rates in 3+ child families.

Figure 7: Percentage reduction in the child poverty rate (% living in households with equivalent income <60% of the median, BHC)

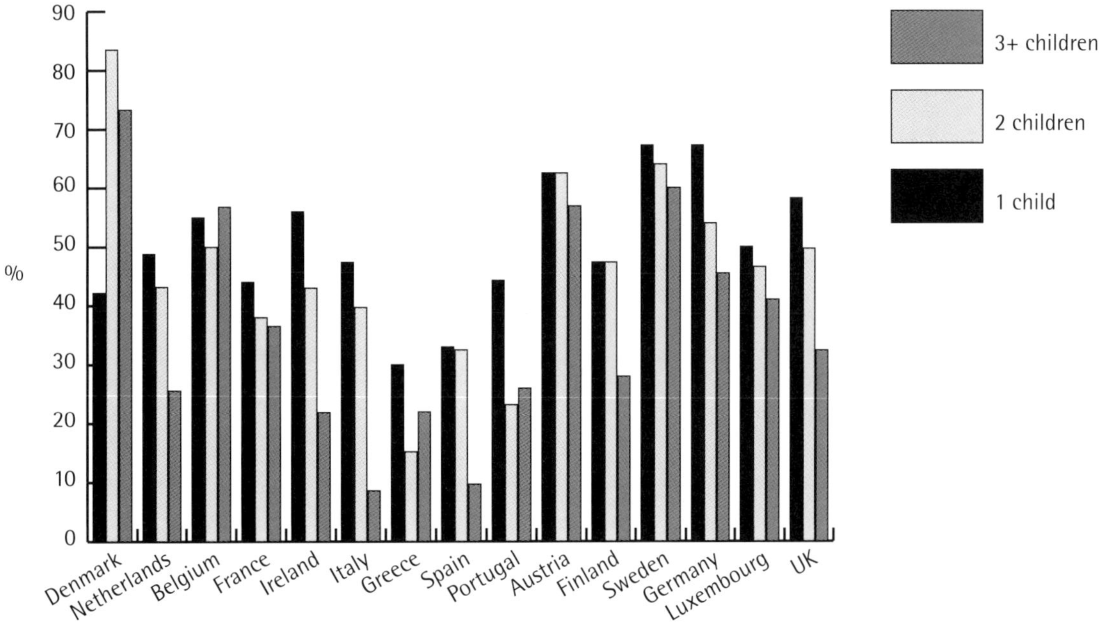

Source: Own analysis of ECHP (2001)

Luxembourg Income Study

The ECHP analysis above is based on the EU15 countries. The LIS enables us to compare the prevalence of child poverty in 23 countries, and how the risks of child poverty vary with the number of children in the family. We also evaluate how countries vary in their provision for families of different sizes by again comparing risks of child poverty before and after benefits.

The LIS is a database of household income surveys for now 29 countries, which provide demographic, income and expenditure information at three different levels: the household, person and child. Each country's survey data is harmonised and standardised in order to facilitate comparative research. The surveys are collated in waves every five years, and the latest wave (wave 5) is used for this analysis, which includes surveys undertaken in 1999/2000.[6] For our analysis we have used the sample of children, and matched the household data to each child. Thus the unit of analysis is the child.

---

[6] 2001 for Israel.

Figure 8 shows the distribution of the number of children living in households. In the UK, 13% of children live in families consisting of four or more children – the sixth highest proportion. The LIS sample size for each country varies, which means that sample sizes are small for 4+ child families in some of our countries. Although, the unweighted number of children in 4+ families does not fall below 50 in any of our countries, we have treated large families as consisting of three or more children for this analysis. In the UK, 37% of children live in families with three or more children, the eighth highest proportion.

We have used a conventional income measure of poverty – children in households falling below 60% of the median income in that country are considered to be poor. We have equivalised income according to the modified OECD equivalence scale. The measure used is BHC. We have measured poverty risks before social benefits (net disposable income – social benefits) and after social benefits (net disposable income). The social benefits accounted for included sick pay, accident pay, disability benefit, social retirement benefits, child and family allowances, unemployment benefits, maternity allowance, military benefits, other social benefits, means-tested cash benefits and near cash benefits. Thus, they do not include tax allowance and credits, which, depending on the emphasis placed on them in a particular country, may have an important effect on the child poverty rate.[7]

Figure 8: Distribution of the number of children living in households

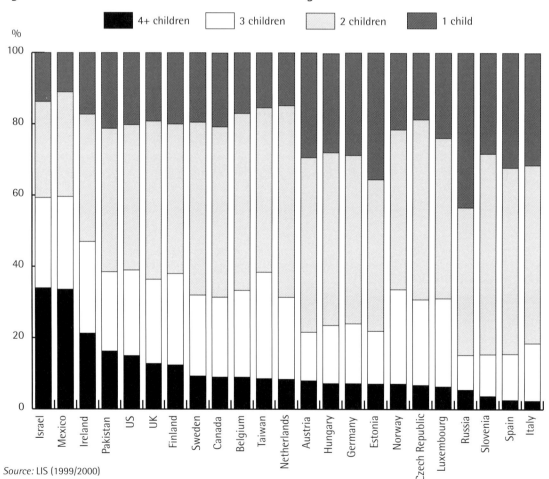

Source: LIS (1999/2000)

---

[7] The UK data is for 1999, before the introduction of Working Families' Tax Credit (WFTC).

We begin by comparing child poverty rates by number of children before social benefits in Figure 9. We can see that, in all our countries, before benefits are taken into account, children in families with three or more children are more likely to be poor compared to children in families with one or two children. The UK has the second worst poverty rate, with 50% of its 3+ child families in poverty before social benefits are accounted for.

Figure 9: Child poverty by number of children before social benefits

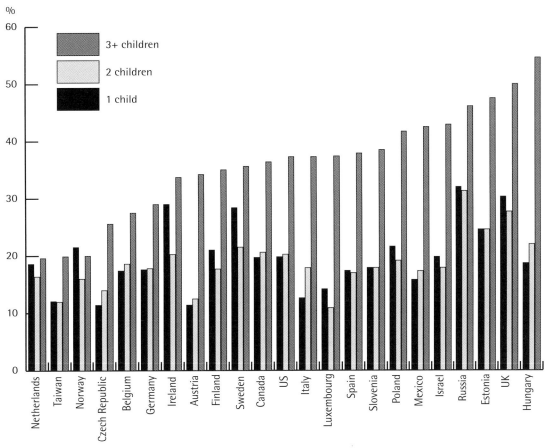

Source: LIS (1999/2000)

Figure 10 shows the child poverty rate by the number of children after social benefits have been taken into account. The UK moves from being the second worst country in terms of child poverty in 3+ child families before social benefits were taken into account to the 10th worst country, with 20% of 3+ child families in poverty.

When we turn our attention to the percentage change in the poverty rate before and after social benefits, as Figure 11 shows, after the Nordic countries, the UK reduces the child poverty rate for 3+ child families by the fourth highest percentage (61%), after social benefits are accounted for. However, the UK is less generous to its 3+ child families vis à vis smaller size families, demonstrated by a smaller percentage reduction in the child poverty rate for 3+ child families after social benefits compared to families with one and two children.

Figure 10: Child poverty by number of children after social benefits

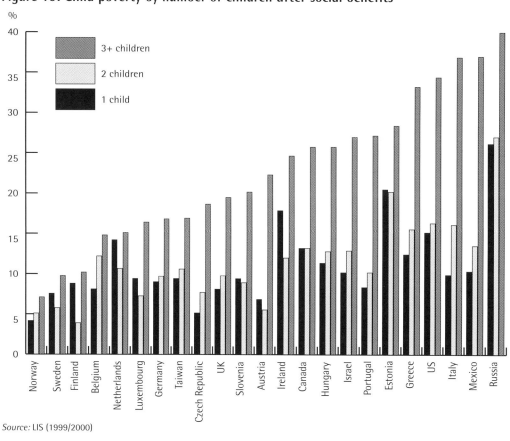

Source: LIS (1999/2000)

Figure 11: Percentage change in child poverty rate before and after social benefits by number of children

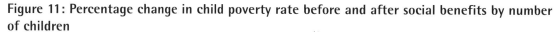
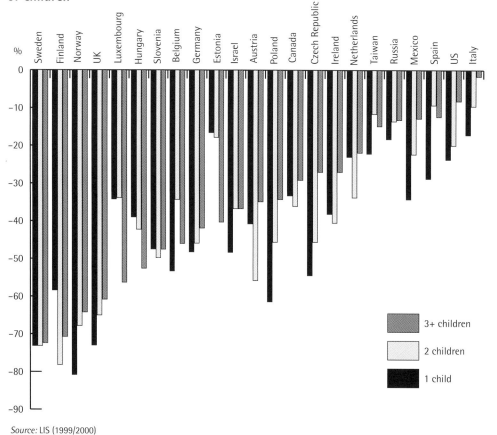

Source: LIS (1999/2000)

Figure 12 shows the difference in the percentage change in the child poverty rate before and after social benefits between families with three or more children and families with one child. If the difference is positive then the percentage change in the poverty rate was greater for 3+ child families than for only-child families; accounting for social benefits reduces the poverty rate by a greater proportion for 3+ child families than for small families. In other words, if the difference is positive then the welfare state is more generous to 3+ child families than to small families. If it is negative then the welfare state is less generous to 3+ child families than small families. Compared to one-child families, the UK is the eighth *least* generous country to 3+ child families, with social benefits reducing the child poverty rate for 3+ child families by 12% *less* than for one-child families.

Figure 12: Difference in percentage change in child poverty rate before and after social benefits between families with three or more children and families with one child

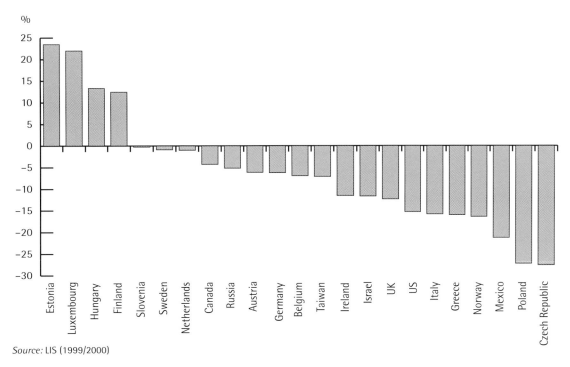

Source: LIS (1999/2000)

So far we have looked at the risks of being poor for families of different sizes. To really understand how different welfare states treat families of different sizes, we need to compare the odds of being poor for children in 3+ child families with children in small families *having controlled for other factors*. To do this we use multivariate logistic regression. Table 22 shows the odds of being poor for two-child and 3+ child households compared to one-child families, holding other factors constant. Unless otherwise noted, the factors held constant are:

- age of the child;
- sex of the child;
- education of the household head;
- earnings composition of the household;
- ethnicity of the household head;
- disability status of the household head;
- tenure status.

Holding other factors constant, we can see that, before benefits are accounted for, in all our countries generally for the 3+ child the family, the greater the odds the child will be poor. In the UK, children in 3+ child families are 4.5 times more likely to be in poverty, the 18th highest odds of all the countries.

Table 22: Odds of being poor for children holding other factors constant[1] by number of children before social benefits, ranked according to the odds of 3+ child families being poor

	1 child	2 children	3+ children
Netherlands[2]	1	NS	NS
Russia	1	NS	1.5*
Taiwan[3]	1	1.5***	2.4***
Israel	1	NS	2.7***
Norway[4]	1	1.3***	2.7***
Slovenia [2]	1	1.6*	2.7***
Sweden	1	1.4***	2.9***
Ireland	1	1.1***	3.0***
Poland[2]	1	1.2*	3.5***
US	1	1.5***	3.5***
Estonia	1	1.4***	3.6***
Czech Republic[5]	1	1.8***	3.8***
Germany	1	1.9***	3.8***
Finland	1	1.2***	4.1***
Spain	1	NS	4.1***
Canada	1	1.6***	4.3***
Mexico[2]	1	1.3***	4.5***
UK	1	1.7***	4.5***
Italy[2]	1	1.7***	4.6***
Belgium	1	4.2***	6.0***
Hungary[2]	1	NS	6.5***
Austria	1	NS	7.9***
Luxembourg	1	1.2**	10.2***

Notes:

***p < 0.001, **p < 0.01, *p < 0.05, NS = not significant.

[1] Factors held constant (unless otherwise stated) are: age of child, sex of child, birth order of child, education of household head, age of household head, earnings composition of the household, ethnicity of the household head, disability status of household head and tenure status.

[2] It was not possible to control for ethnicity since this variable was not available in the country dataset.

[3] It was not possible to control for ethnicity nor disability since these variables were not available in the country dataset.

[4] It was not possible to control for tenure since this variable was not available in the country dataset.

[5] It was not possible to control for disability since this variable was not available in the country dataset.

Source: LIS (1999/2000)

Table 23 shows the percentage change in the odds of being poor for children, holding other factors constant, by number of children[8] before and after social benefits. We can see that, holding other factors constant, the effect of social benefits for the majority of the countries was to reduce the odds of poverty for 3+ child families vis à vis one-child families. In the UK, children in 3+ child families enjoyed the seventh greatest reduction in the odds of being poor compared to one-child families, with policy reducing their odds of being poor by 51%.

Table 23: Percentage change in the odds of being poor for children holding other factors constant[1] by number of children before and after social benefits, ranked according to the change in the odds of 3+ child families

	2 children (%)	3+ children (%)
Russia	NC	BNS
Slovenia[2]	BNS	BNS
Luxembourg	-33	-82
Finland	-58	-71
Estonia	-14	-61
Austria	NC	-59
UK	-24	-51
Sweden	-21	-45
Hungary[2]	NC	-42
Israel	BS	-41
Belgium	-29	-38
Germany	-21	-37
Ireland	NC	-10
Mexico[2]	-8	-4
Spain	BS	NC
Netherlands[2]	NC	NC
Taiwan[4]	7	NC
Canada	-6	7
Czech Republic[3]	NC	8
US	NC	9
Norway[5]	38	11
Poland[2]	25	14
Italy[2]	6	20

Notes:

NC = no change in the odds or remained not significant; BNS = became not significant; BS = became significant

[1] Factors held constant (unless otherwise stated) are: age of child, sex of child, birth order of child, education of household head, age of household head, earnings composition of the household, ethnicity of the household head, disability status of household head and tenure status.

[2] It was not possible to control for ethnicity since this variable was not available in the country dataset.

[3] It was not possible to control for tenure since this variable was not available in the country dataset.

[4] It was not possible to control for either ethnicity or disability since these variables were not available in the country dataset.

[5] It was not possible to control for disability since this variable was not available in the country dataset.

Source: LIS (1999/2000)

---

[8]   Some of the variation by the number of children may be due to variation by age – the age assumptions of children in the model families were two years and 11 months, and 7, 14 and 17 years.

These comparative analyses using two independent data sets show that the UK has one of the highest pre-transfer poverty rates for children in 3+ child families compared to other countries. However, it appears that the UK is average in the generosity of the benefit package to 3+ child families. However, starting from a relatively high pre-transfer rate, UK policy is fairly effective in reducing its 3+ child family child poverty rate and the chances of poverty for children in 3+ child families. However, the UK is not the most generous country, and children in 3+ child families still experience greater risks of poverty than children in smaller families. Thus, the UK is doing relatively well for its 3+ child families, but could do better.

6

The treatment of family size in the Child Benefit package: comparisons with other countries

This chapter uses comparative data to explore how the Child Benefit (CB) packages of different countries treat families with different numbers of children. All industrialised countries have a package of tax benefits, cash benefits, exemptions from charges, subsidies and services in kind which assist parents with the costs of raising children. This package plays a part, along with labour market income, in tackling market-driven child poverty and we compared earlier how child poverty is mitigated by elements of this package.

We know from the series of studies that we have undertaken over the years (Bradshaw and Finch, 2002) that countries structure their packages to take account of the needs of families of different types and sizes, some take account of the age of the child, many vary their package by earnings and the package also varies according to whether childcare and housing costs are taken into account. In this analysis we are primarily concerned with how the package varies with the number of children in a family. We draw on two studies – the Bradshaw and Finch (2002) study that covered the packages of 22 countries including the UK in July 2001 and the Bradshaw and Mayhew (2005) study that covered 15 countries including the UK in January 2004. The analysis is based on an estimate of what a variety of model families would be entitled to in each country. The models assume certain characteristics of the families and their earnings. The method is designed to ensure that like is being compared with like. The results are illustrative, not representative. They present a formal picture of how policies *should* operate given the law and regulations, not necessarily how they *do* operate. In particular, no allowance is made for non-take-up of income-tested cash benefits or tax benefits. Also, after the impact of the package, families have to pay different prices for commodities, and in some countries they have to pay for services that are free or subsidised in other countries.

We start by summarising the situation in 2001. Figure 13 takes a standard one-earner family on average earnings and shows how the CB package varies in 22 countries with the number of children in each country, with a childless couple set to 100. The chart shows the percentage addition that families with children receive over and above the net income of a childless couple on the same earnings. It is therefore a measure of the effort made by states to support children. The UK is unique in all these countries in having CB that pays a higher rate for the first child in the family, so it is comparatively generous to a one-child family; it is far less generous to a three-child family compared with other countries.

Figure 13: Child Benefit package by number of children, July 2001. Childless couple = 100

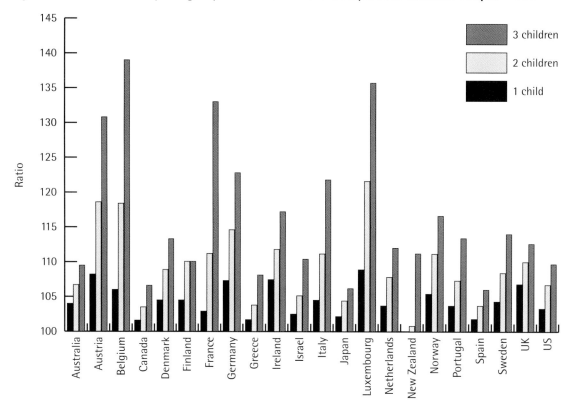

Source: Bradshaw and Finch (2002)

Table 24 provides data on how the value of the CB package varies with the number (and ages)[10] of the children. The left hand side of the table takes the tax and cash benefit part of the package. A number of countries pay the same, or virtually the same, amount per child – Australia, Canada, Denmark, Finland, Greece, Japan, the Netherlands, Spain, and the US. Ireland and the UK pay higher amounts for the first child in the family. France pays much less for the first child. Belgium, France, Germany, Israel, Italy, New Zealand and Portugal pay higher amounts for the third (and subsequent) child. There is clearly very little international agreement about the implied equivalence in these patterns of variation. The right hand side of the table shows how the CB package varies by the number of children after housing costs and services have been taken into account. The countries that are now relatively more generous to larger families are Austria, Belgium and France. The UK package for three-child families compared to a childless couple comes 11th in the league table of 22 countries.

Table 24 gives the implied equivalence scale for the tax benefit package for a family in employment. Using data collected in the study we are also able to explore the implied equivalence scale of families receiving social assistance (see Table 25). After tax and cash benefits only the implied equivalence scale for a three-child family compared with a childless couple is highest of all 22 countries in the UK. After housing costs and services the UK comes ninth. This of course does not imply that social assistance for large families is comparatively generous – just that it is comparatively generous to families with children compared with a childless couple. In fact the social assistance scales paid to a couple with three children in the UK in pounds sterling purchasing power parity is seventh highest out of 22 countries.

---

[10] Some of the variation by the number of children may be due to variation by age – the age assumptions of children in the model families were 2 years and 11 months, 7, 14 and 17.

Table 24: Variation in Child Benefit package by number of children. Childless couple = 100. One-earner average male earnings, July 2001

Country	After tax and cash benefits only			After taxes and cash benefits, housing costs and services		
	Couple +1 child aged 7	Couple +2 children aged 7 and 14	Couple +3 children aged 7, 14 and 17	Couple +1 child aged 7	Couple +2 children aged 7 and 14	Couple +3 children aged 7, 14 and 17
Australia	104	107	110	105	108	111
Austria	108	119	131	111	124	161
Belgium	106	118	139	108	123	151
Canada	102	104	107	101	103	106
Denmark	104	109	113	106	115	124
Finland	105	110	110	113	128	134
France	103	111	133	103	117	158
Germany	107	115	123	111	122	135
Greece	102	104	108	95	89	81
Ireland	108	112	117	107	110	114
Israel	103	105	110	102	103	111
Italy	105	111	122	106	113	124
Japan	102	104	106	100	97	94
Luxembourg	109	122	136	110	124	141
Netherlands	104	108	112	100	98	90
New Zealand	100	100	111	99	99	113
Norway	106	111	117	108	115	120
Portugal	104	107	114	96	94	98
Spain	102	104	106	101	103	106
Sweden	104	109	114	111	121	134
UK	107	110	113	110	112	116
US	103	107	110	96	92	88

Source: Bradshaw and Finch (2002)

Table 25: Implied equivalence scale of social assistance. Childless couple = 100, July 2001

Country	After tax and cash benefits only			After taxes and cash benefits, housing costs and services		
	Couple +1 child aged 7	Couple +2 children aged 7 and 14	Couple +3 children aged 7, 14 and 17	Couple +1 child aged 7	Couple +2 children aged 7 and 14	Couple +3 children aged 7, 14 and 17
Australia	1.31	1.55	1.55	1.58	1.99	2.43
Austria	1.33	1.74	2.21	1.49	2.10	2.68
Belgium	1.18	1.45	1.78	1.36	1.34	1.92
Canada	1.35	1.73	2.12	2.55	4.27	5.99
Denmark	1.33	1.39	1.46	1.54	1.64	1.73
Finland	1.28	1.62	1.93	1.51	2.03	2.52
France	1.23	1.51	2.04	1.47	2.20	3.30
Germany	1.30	1.70	2.24	1.30	1.70	2.24
Ireland	1.32	1.63	2.01	1.33	1.66	2.05
Israel	1.29	1.59	1.76	1.73	2.19	2.47
Italy	0.75	0.88	1.02	0.49	0.71	0.87
Japan	1.29	1.67	2.03	1.66	2.46	3.36
Luxembourg	1.18	1.43	1.75	1.24	1.58	2.06
Netherlands	1.09	1.18	1.27	1.13	1.22	1.34
New Zealand	1.25	1.37	1.58	1.24	1.39	1.65
Norway	0.95	1.13	1.30	1.29	1.59	1.83
Portugal	1.34	1.69	2.18	1.81	2.64	3.77
Spain	1.20	1.38	1.56	1.57	1.90	2.27
Sweden	0.97	1.12	1.30	1.32	1.68	2.08
UK	1.55	1.93	2.32	1.63	2.06	2.46
US	1.29	1.58	1.86	2.58	4.24	4.20

Source: Bradshaw and Finch (2002)

We have recently replicated the model family analysis for 15 countries as at January 2004 (Bradshaw, 2006: forthcoming). Figure 14 shows how the CB package varies by the number of children in the family – for couples and keeping earnings constant. In New Zealand only the three-child family receives any more than a childless couple. The other countries are making rather different judgements about the relative needs of families of different sizes. Austria is more generous for the third child and so are Belgium and Sweden to a lesser extent. Australia is more generous to the second child and the UK is still unusual in favouring the first child.

Figure 14: Child Benefit package by number of children. Childless couple = 100. Average earnings after tax, benefits and housing subsidies

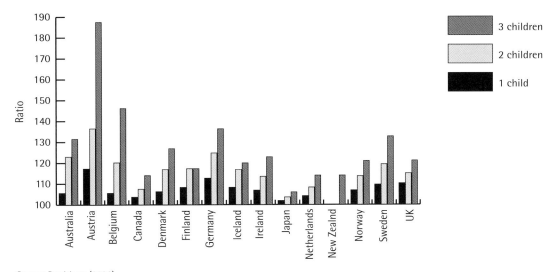

Source: Bradshaw (2006)

7

Modelling policy changes for large families

The government has an aspiration to improve the financial support available to large families. How might it achieve this and at what cost? This section uses a micro-simulation model of the tax and benefit system (POLIMOD, with the assistance of Professor Holly Sutherland from the University of Essex) in an attempt to answer those questions.

The version of POLIMOD used is based on the 1999/2000 Family Resources Survey (FRS) with incomes updated to 2005/06 prices and incomes using a method documented in Sutherland (2004) and used in Sutherland et al (2003). Further updating has occurred since then, using the same basic methods. Policy parameters are those for October 2005. At the time the analysis was undertaken new Income Support (IS) cases with children were being taken onto Child Tax Credit (CTC) but existing cases had not been transferred. In the modelling we have assumed that all IS cases are on CTC. The main effect of doing this is that all families on IS do see Child Benefit (CB) increases as well as CTC increases. Poverty is measured as having a household income below 60% of median household disposable income. Incomes are equivalised using the modified Organisation for Economic Co-operation and Development (OECD) equivalence scale and before housing costs (BHC) income measures are used.

Six policy changes were simulated. The latter two are designed to be revenue neutral to the Exchequer:

- **Policy change 1:** Set CB for all children to be the same level as the first child (£17.00). All families with 2+ children better off by £5.60 per second and subsequent child.
- **Policy change 2:** As policy change 1 but also add £5 per child for third and subsequent children. One-child families: no change; two-child families better off by £5.60; three-child families better off by £16.20 (2 x £5.60 + £5) and so on.
- **Policy change 3:** As policy change 1 but also add £20 per child for third and subsequent children. One-child families: no change; two-child families better off by £5.60; three-child families better off by £31.20 (2 x £5.60 + £20) and so on.
- **Policy change 4:** As policy change 1 but levelling up CTC, Housing Benefit (HB) and Council Tax Benefit (CTB) so that the amount for all children is the same as the first. This is modelled by retaining the family premia and adding the same amount to the per child payments for second and subsequent children. There is no effective size-specific extra payment in this run. This means that there are no losers and that all 2+ child families gain. Those on IS or maximum CTC gain about £11 per child for the second and subsequent child.
- **Policy change 5:** As policy change 2 but also abolish family premia in CTC, HB and CTB and add £10 to the per child amounts for third and subsequent children. In order for it to be revenue neutral £1.34 has been added to each child's CB. Families with 3+ children gain from this and those with two or fewer mostly lose because the CB increase is not sufficient to cover the cost of losing the CTC family premium. This applies whether or not the family has a low or middle income.

- **Policy change 6:** As policy change 5 but add £20 per child for third and subsequent children and make it revenue neutral by increasing CB by £0.70 per week.

Educational Maintenance Allowances are not included in any of these simulations.

Table 26 provides a summary of the revenue costs of these policy changes and the proportion of gainers and losers.

The effect on child poverty rates is shown in Table 27. The best outcome in terms of equity for large families is achieved by policy change 3. The child poverty rate in large families is now similar to small families. This policy change results in a very small increase in the child poverty rate of lone parents with one child; all other groups gain. However, policy change 3 is the most expensive of the options considered, costing an extra £3.39 billion. Policy changes 1 and 2 achieve more modest reductions in the poverty rates of large families but at lower costs. Policy change 4 also does well for large families and costs less than policy change 3 – because it uses CTC rather than CB it is slightly less expensive. Policy changes 5 and 6 also use CTC but they are made revenue neutral by abolishing the family element in CTC and increasing CBs across the board. Most of improvements in the child poverty rate of large families are paid for by losses for better-off families. However, not all and there is a slight increase in the child poverty rates in small families overall and especially small lone-parent families.

Table 26: Revenue costs, gainers and losers of policy simulations

Policy change	Net cost £bn/year	% households with children gaining	% households with children losing
1	1.62	59	–
2	2.06	59	–
3	3.39	59	–
4	3.06	59	–
5	0	30	69
6	0	31	69

Source: Analysis of POLIMOD

Table 27: Effect on child poverty rates – BHC (OECD Modified Scale)

Policy changes	Baseline	1	2	3	4	5	6
All child family	19.2	16.9	15.9	14.1	13.3	17.0	16.3
1-child family	15.3	15.3	15.3	15.3	15.4	17.3	17.4
2-child family	14.9	13.4	13.4	13.4	11.3	15.7	16.0
3-child family	23.2	19.1	17.5	14.2	13.8	16.6	15.2
4-child family	30.8	24.7	22.4	14.1	14.6	22.0	16.5
5+child family	40.9	34.8	24.2	13.2	18.5	22.2	20.3
Lone parent 1 child	30.7	30.8	30.8	30.8	30.8	35.0	35.1
Lone parent 2 children	34.0	28.4	28.4	28.4	20.0	36.2	36.9
Lone parent 3+ children	38.2	27.1	22.2	15.5	14.7	19.8	17.2
Couple 1 child	9.1	9.1	9.1	9.1	9.3	10.2	10.4
Couple 2 children	10.0	9.5	9.5	9.5	9.1	10.3	10.5
Couple 3+ children	23.4	20.6	18.5	13.6	14.5	18.0	15.7

Source: Analysis of POLIMOD

These results illustrate that policy makers seeking to help large families face trade-offs of three kinds:

- About half of all poor children live in one- or two-child families and any policy which helps large families at the expense of small families is likely to result in an increase in child poverty in small families and also probably lone parent families (who are mainly small) and thus also possibly an increase in child poverty overall.
- There is, of course, a trade-off between the effectiveness of the policy in terms of equity and the costs.
- There are also choices to be made between universal and selective policy measures. Improvements in CBs for large families are expensive because they go to every large family whatever their income. Manipulating CTC for large families may concentrate extra help on those who need it most. However, it may suffer from non-take-up and may also increase the poverty trap (high marginal tax rates as earnings rise).

In any case a factor that might also be an important constraint on policy is the general public's views about the deserts of large families and/or the actual or believed behavioural or fertility effects of paying enhanced benefits to large families. An enhanced benefit for one-child families raises no objections because every family with a child has at least one child. However, if an enhanced benefit is to be paid for the third and subsequent children, smaller (and childless) families may object. There will certainly be arguments about the relative needs of families with different numbers of children and probably anxiety expressed about the extent to which such premiums might be encouraging 'irresponsible' childbirth.

Conclusion

The UK government is committed to the eradication of child poverty by 2020. Large families have a higher risk of poverty than small families. In 2003/04, 51% of children in 4+ child families were poor compared with only 24% in one-child families. Children in 3+ child families constituted 41% of all poor children. If the policy is to be achieved then attention needs to be paid to larger families.

Parents of children in large families are different in their character and most of these differences are associated with a higher risk of child poverty. But there is still a large-family effect independent of these characteristics. This is because wages are not adjusted to the number of children a wage earner has to support and the UK Child Benefit (CB) package is at present geared to small families. This is a unique characteristic – no other countries that vary their CB package provide more help to small families. The UK poverty rate for large families is among the highest in the OECD.

The Child Poverty Review announced 'a long-term aspiration to improve the financial support available to large families' (HM Treasury, 2004, p 6). Long-term implies that it will be achieved by gearing benefit rates towards larger families over a period of years. Child Benefit and/or Child Tax Credits could be geared to reducing child poverty in large families but there is a trade-off between Exchequer costs and selectivity.

There are difficult policy choices to be made if the government is to meet its target to eradicate child poverty. Attention will need to be focused at some point on large families. There are also strong social justice arguments for our tax benefit system being more sensitive to large families.

References

Adelman, L., Middleton, S. and Ashworth, K. (2003) *Britain's poorest children: Severe and persistent poverty and social exclusion*, London: Save the Children.

Anderson, E.S. (1999) 'What is the point of equality?', *Ethics*, vol 109, no 2, pp 287-337.

Baldwin, S. and Cooke, K. (1984) *How much is enough? A review of supplementary scale rates*, London: Family Policy Studies Centre.

Berthoud, R. and Ford, R. (1996) *Relative needs: Variations in the living standards of different types of households*, London: Policy Studies Institute.

Berthoud, R. and Iacovou, M. (2006) *The economic position of large families*, DWP Research Report, London: DWP.

Berthoud, R., Bryan, M. and Bardasi, E. (2004) *The dynamics of deprivation: The relationship between income and material deprivation over time*, DWP Research Report No. 219, Leeds: Corporate Document Services.

Bradshaw, J. (2006) 'Child Benefit packages in fifteen countries', in J. Lewis, *Children, changing families and welfare states*, Cheltenham: Edward Elgar.

Bradshaw, J. and Finch, N. (2002) *A comparison of child benefit packages in 22 countries*, Department for Work and Pensions Research Report No.174, Leeds: Corporate Document Services.

Bradshaw, J. and Lynes, T. (1995) *Benefit uprating policy and living standards*, SPRU Social Policy Report No. 1, York: Social Policy Research Unit, University of York.

Bradshaw, J. and Mayhew, E. (eds) (2005) *The well-being of children in the United Kingdom*, London: Save the Children.

Bradshaw, J., Mayhew, E., Dex, S., Joshi, H. and Ward, K. (2005) 'Socioeconomic origins of parents and child poverty', in S. Dex and H. Joshi (eds) *Children of the 21st century: From birth to nine months*, Bristol: The Policy Press, pp 71-108.

Cantillon, B. and Van den Bosch, K. (2002) 'Social policy strategies to combat income poverty of children and families in Europe', LIS Working Paper No. 336 (www.lisproject.org/publications/liswps/336.pdf).

DWP (Department for Work and Pensions) (2004a) *The abstract of statistics*, available at: www.dwp.gov.uk/asd/asd1/abstract/Abstract2003.pdf

DWP (2004b) *Tax benefit model tables: April 2004*, available at: www.dwp.gov.uk/asd/asd1/TBMT_2004.pdf

DWP (2005) *Household below average incomes 2003/04*, Leeds: Corporate Document Services.

DWP (2006) *Household below average incomes 2004/05*, Leeds: Corporate Document Services.

Ermisch, J. and Francesconi, M. (2001) 'Family matters: impacts of family background on educational attainments', *Economica*, vol 68, no 270, pp 137-56.

Field, F. (1985) *What price a child?*, London: Policy Studies Institute.

Ford, R. (1997) *Estimating relative needs through a comparison of living standards*, London: Policy Studies Institute.

Gordon, D., Levitas, R., Pantazis, C., Patsios, D., Payne, S., Townsend, P., Adelman, L., Ashworth, K., Middleton, S., Bradshaw, J. and Williams, J. (2000) *Poverty and social exclusion in Britain*, York: Joseph Rowntree Foundation.

Gregg, P. and Machin, S. (2001) 'Childhood experiences, educational attainment and adult labour market performance', in K. Vleminckx and T.M. Smeeding (eds) *Child well-being, child poverty and child policy in modern nations*, Bristol: The Policy Press pp 129-50.

HM Treasury (2000) *Spending review 2002: Public service agreements 2001-2004*, Cm 4808, London: The Stationery Office.

HM Treasury (2002) *Technical note for HM Treasury's Public Service Agreement 2003-2006*, London: HM Treasury.

HM Treasury (2004) *Child poverty review*, London: HM Treasury.

Hobcraft, J. and Kiernan, K. (2001) 'Childhood poverty, early motherhood and adult social exclusion', *British Journal of Sociology*, vol 52, no 3, pp 495-517.

Iacovou, M. (2001) 'Family composition and children's educational outcomes', Working Paper 2001-12, Colchester: Institute for Social and Economic Research, Essex University.

Kemp, P., Bradshaw, J., Dornan, P., Finch, N. and Mayhew, E. (2004) *Routes out of poverty: A research review*, York: Joseph Rowntree Foundation.

Land, H. (1969) *Large families in London*, Occasional Papers on Social Administration No. 32, London: G. Bell & Sons Ltd.

Layte, R. and Fouage, D. (2004) 'The dynamics of income poverty', in R. Berthoud and M. Iacovou (eds) *Social Europe, living standards and welfare states*, Cheltenham: Edward Elgar.

McLaughlin, E. and Byrne, B. (2005) *Disability and equality: Themes of sameness and difference in policy, theories and practice*, Equality and Social Inclusion in Ireland Project, Working Paper No. 9, Belfast: Queen's University Belfast.

Mayhew, E. and Bradshaw, J. (2005) 'Mothers, babies and the risks of poverty', *Poverty*, 121, pp 13-16.

National Statistics (2005) *Social Trends, No 35, 2005 Edition*, Basingstoke: Palgrave Macmillan.

ONS (Office for National Statistics) (2003) *Population trends No. 113*, London: ONS.

Rathbone, E. (1949) *Family allowances: A new edition of the disinherited family*, London: George Allen and Unwin.

Redmond, G. (2000) *Children in large families: Disadvantaged or just different?*, LIS Working Paper No. 225 (www.lisproject.org/publications/liswps/225.pdf).

Sutherland, H. (2004) *Poverty in Britain: the impact of government policy since 1997: a projection to 2004-5 using microsimulation*, Microsimulation Research Note MU/RN/44 (www.iser.essex.ac.uk/msu/publications/pdf/murn44.pdf).

Sutherland, H., Sefton, T. and Piachaud, D. (2003) *Poverty in Britain: The impact of government policy since 1997*, York: Joseph Rowntree Foundation.

Townsend, P. (1979) *Poverty in the United Kingdom*, London: Penguin Books.

Vegeris, S. and Perry, J. (2003) *Families and Children Study 2001: Living standards and the children*, DWP Research Report No. 190, Leeds: Corporate Document Services.

Whelan, C., Layte, R. and Maitre, B. (2004) 'Deprivation and social exclusion', in R. Berthoud and M. Iacovou (eds) *Social Europe, living standards and welfare states*, Cheltenham: Edward Elgar.

Willitts, M. and Swales, K. (2003) *Characteristics of large families*, IAD, Social Research Division, DWP in-house report (www.dwp.gov.uk/asd/asd5/ih2003-2004/IH118.pdf).